CONCILIUM

Religion in the Seventies

CONCILIUM

Concilium 117 (7/1978): Canon Law

THE FINANCES
OF
THE CHURCH

Edited by

William Bassett and
Peter Huizing

A CROSSROAD BOOK

The Seabury Press · New York

1979
The Seabury Press
815 Second Avenue
New York, N.Y. 10017

Library of Congress Catalog Card Number: 79-83933
ISBN: 0-8164-0407-0
ISBN: 0-8164-2197-8 (pbk.)
Printed in the United States of America

CONTENTS

Part III
Bulletins

Editorial

IN THE Catholic Church financial administration in the strict sense refers to the management of sums of money and economic or pecuniarily appreciable goods belonging to ecclesiastical institutions such as parishes, dioceses, ecclesiastical provinces and foundations: in short, ecclesiastical corporations in the legal sense.

Early medieval authors attributed the ownership of such property to the patron saints of these corporations. The charters of legacies and donations to such corporations named the patron saints as the beneficiaries. The fortune of the diocese of Rome was described as the property of St Peter—*patrimonium sancti Petri*. This is the way in which the faithful expressed symbolically their sense of justice: the earthly administrators—parish priests, bishops, popes, abbots, and so on—had to manage these goods in the interests of the respective corporations, and the patron saints had to watch this. The canonists of the late Middle Ages saw the institutions as the subjects of their respective wealth and responsible for the rights and obligations linked with it, and therefore as 'legal persons.' By this they meant that the managers could not act in their own name or person, but in the name or the 'person,' and therefore, in the interest of the institution.

The way in which ecclesiastical institutions acquire their revenue, and administer and spend it, has a considerable effect on the social presence of the Church and the churches and the image people have of them. The credibility of the churches depends for a large part on the way in which ecclesiastical institutions behave in the socio-economic sector. These ways have varied considerably from one age to another. This was partly because, in so far as transactions of money and property are concerned, these institutions had to play along with the social and economic structures of the day, even if they were critical of them. Franciscan poverty could only maintain itself in a structure where the poor for God's sake could count on sufficient support from the burghers to be sure of at least a minimal livelihood.

This Concilium offers information about church finances today.

The first section describes some typical systems of church finance. Information is given as fully as the limits of one issue allow about the finances of the Vatican, particularly in so far as paying for the Vatican itself is concerned (Cereti). The reason is that precisely in this field carelessness or even a tendency to shy away from publicity encourages what is feared most: vague unrealistic suspicions and slanted journalism. The financial basis of the Churches in the Federal Republic (BRD) and the North American Churches (USA) which are deemed to be the wealthiest churches within the Catholic Church (and carry the burden of this situation) is quite different.

Ecclesiastical economics in the BRD relies on the church tax (*Kirchensteuer*). This is a surtax mainly on capital and income, imposed and collected by the State on behalf of the Church (Walf). In the United States the Church has to rely on voluntary contributions by the faithful, although in recent years indirect support by the States and the Federal Government has become indispensable, particularly in education and health (Bassett). For the responsible acquisition of funds, a vital source of revenue for ecclesiastical institutions in the United States, the bishops and the major superiors of female and male religious laid down some basic principles and guidelines in 1977 (McManus). Unfortunately, a promised contribution of the Church in Spain as typical of a 'national Church' failed to turn up. The contributions of the Church in Poland, as typical of a Church in a country ruled by Communists (Schmitz), and of the Orthodox Churches in the Near East (Nikitopoulos) tell us more about the general than the financial situation of these Churches, and for that reason have been put into the 'bulletin' section. The first section finishes with an exposé of revenue, spending and financial administration in the context of an international religious order or congregation.

The second section contains articles on some more general aspects and problems in the field of church finance.

In the Churches' contribution to development aid the mainly charitable kind of aid has gradually been turned into aid that is integrated in political activity in order to influence public opinion, particularly in industrialized nations. The idea was to make people see that the introduction of purely technological industrial development into 'underdeveloped' by 'developed' countries merely creates progressive disintegration in both. Is there a chance that, within the international context of the Christian Churches, the 'older' Churches will recognize the right of self-determination of the 'younger' Churches in such a way that they could contribute to more just relationships between the nations and a new and just order of legal rights at the international level (Cosmao)? Co-operation and communion between the Churches could be really productive here if inspired by the determination to achieve a liberation which goes beyond liberation from lack of money or material goods (Rood).

The whole field of church finance, from the Vatican to the religious

orders and congregations, shows the pressure caused by the apparently
insoluble coupling of the financial-economic structure of church institutions with the capitalistic structure of the world's economy, imposed
by the dominant economic and political power structures. By this we
mean the economy in which the participating powers want, each for
itself, to expand their own possessions and their own power. The result
is inevitably the progressive disintegration of the world economy. Can
the Church, can the churches, imprisoned in this structure, still honour
their traditional function as 'stewards of the poor'? As long as the
wealthy churches have to spend a vast part of their revenue on their
own major institutions and the ensured welfare of their personnel,
leaving only a very modest percentage for aid to poor churches and
countries, they cannot possibly fulfil this function. Can we hope that
the already clearly effective breaking down of powerful ecclesiastical
institutions and the impoverishment of wealthy churches will really
spark off the determination of the whole of Christianity to break
through the capitalistic world-economy and to achieve a more fraternal
relationship between the nations (Trouiller)? Cereti suggests that a re-
orientation of the 'service of St Peter' might well save the Vatican
considerable expense if it were content with functioning as a spiritual
and moral centre rather than as an organization for government and
control, and that in this perspective a critical examination of the ways
in which the various bodies of the Curia and the nunciatures function is
most desirable. This suggestion might be heeded by other churches.
Bassett's complaint that Catholics are overburdened with administrative and institutional affairs and that there are too many pastors but too
few prophets, social critics and mystics among the clergy does not only
apply to the Church in the United States. Moreover, the 'sharing' of
the churches among themselves and with the poor should not be
cramped by too much independence of the autonomous units of the
Church's wealth. This leaves the management in the dioceses as well as
in the religious orders too limited possibilities of effectively promoting
this sharing (Boyle). Nor should it be hampered by what canon law
lays down regarding the alienation of church property; this over-
emphasizes the security of the church institutions themselves but gives
practically no thought to the function of church property as the property of the poor (Bassett). There *are* practical ways which lead to a
'Church of the poor.' Church property is the property of ecclesiastical
institutions, never the private property of one or more persons. Clergy
and, with certain limitations, most religious can certainly have private
possessions but that is not church property. The financial administration of ecclesiastical wealth is therefore always meant to serve the
interests of the community. Moreover, church institutions appeal for,
and largely live by, revenue brought in by the church community.

Administrators of church property are responsible to the community for the administration and use of this property.

The nervousness with which canon law clings to the rule that the ordained president of the community (parish priest, bishop) must have exclusive power in deciding financial matters of parish or diocese whereas others, lay people included, can only function in an advisory capacity, might perhaps be explained as a remnant from the Church's struggle against powers with a greedy eye on church affairs, but it certainly has no basis in theology or canon law. The revived religious awareness of collective responsibility as well as today's demand for responsible financial administration require that decisions be taken collectively, and that expertise should be looked for in properly trained and experienced lay people rather than among the clergy.

The article on the rôle of the laity (Bayerlein) has been written from a West German angle but its motivation has a much wider range. In the same way the article on the care for the sick and the aged (Brion) has been written from the French angle but it outlines a broader development: namely, the transition from clergy and religious working in their own religious and diocesan institutions to working in ordinary service on a contractual basis with independent institutions. With this goes the transition from caring for the sick and the aged in a diocesan and religious context to taking part in the general social system of medical and geriatric service.

For many priests who can get no pay for their own work or from the community in which they live, mass stipends are still the only way of providing for themselves, however modestly. This is not a matter of ecclesiastical financial administration but we include an article on finance and fees for the administration of the sacraments. This sets out the present understanding of stipends and their legitimacy (Kilmartin).

WILLIAM BASSETT
PETER HUIZING

PART I

Financial Structures in the Church:
Comparative Studies

Giovanni Cereti

The Financial Resources and Activities
of the Vatican

AN OLD Roman tradition claims that the deacon Laurence was burned alive on 10 August 258, after the Imperial authorities had failed to snatch the treasures of the Christian community in Rome from him. Laurence distributed these to the needy of the community, and then showed the prefect the poor, saying that these should constitute the true and only treasure of the Church of Christ.

Whatever the historical basis for this story, it shows that already in the course of the early centuries of the Church of Rome, its possessions were reputed to be considerable, but what it shows above all is the conviction that such possessions belonged in the first place to the poor. The theme of the Church's possessions as the patrimony of the poor appears constantly in the early Church.[1] By the end of the fifth century it was solidly established that the Church's goods should, on principle, be divided into four parts: for the bishop, the clergy, 'good works' and the poor. To this end, the patrimony of the Church should be administered in such a way that it could easily be supervised by the Christian people.

It was not till the advent of feudal mentality and customs that the administration of the Church's goods, which had continued to grow as a result of bequests, particularly of land, was reserved to those in positions of authority, while the rest of the people were reduced to a state in which they could no longer exercise any control. In Rome in particular, the administration was placed under the control of trusted henchmen of the pope, who were invested with wide-ranging powers: these were the *Camera thesauraria* of the eleventh century, the *Camerarius* of the twelfth and the *Thesaurarius* of the thirteenth. To face up to the growing need for a papacy that could still play a rôle equal to the growing secular powers, particularly in the thirteenth and fourteenth centuries, the Roman curia increased its fund-raising activities enormously, using the reserves created mainly for the bestowal of benefices. This fiscal system produced understandable resentment and outright opposition. Then, as everyone remembers, came the preaching of indulgences for the building of the basilica of St Peter, which brought such great damage to Christianity.

This historical inheritance explains why for so many centuries the behaviour of the Holy See in the economic field has been regarded with suspicion and mistrust, to the point of being a stumbling-block to the faith of many. Even today there are many, especially among the young and in the poor countries of the world, who feel real disgust when they hear accounts of all the 'treasures' in the Vatican; who regard all the pomp and circumstance and the apparent triumphalism of the great structures surrounding the See of Peter as an undesirable remnant of the past; who question the advisability of the involvement of the Holy See in the capitalist system through the investments it has made and still holds, in equity, bonds and property, in the rich countries of the Western world. The secrecy in which the Vatican's accounts and income are also wrapped not only appears in increasing contrast to the expression of an ecclesiology of communion, but gives rise to rumours of all sorts about the riches of the Vatican, which damage the image of the Holy See and of the pope himself in the eyes of the world at large.

In order to shed a little light on the problem, let us first of all see how the financial administration of the Vatican is organized, then what choices in the economic field have faced the Church in the last few years, and finally ask what the prospects are for the future.

To set the limits of this investigation: it looks at the revenues from the goods owned or administered by the Holy See, which term includes not only the pope and all the bodies that help him in the service he renders to the Universal Church (Can. 7, *C.J.C.*), but also those bodies serving the pope as sovereign of the Vatican City State, those that help him in his capacity of Bishop of Rome, and other bodies directly dependent on the Holy See. The close connections existing between the administrations of these different bodies, as well as their common sharing of expenses, prevents distinctions being made in practice, though they should theoretically be possible. The possessions of dioceses other than Rome, of parishes, religious orders, and congregations, and various Church institutes, whatever control the Holy See exercises over them, must remain outside the scope of this enquiry.

Canon 1518 reads: 'Romanus Pontifex est omnium bonorum eccle-siasticorum supremus administrator et dispensator.' This, however, is a statement of principle belonging to the date when the *Codex* was promulgated, with no practical consequences. The fact that the Holy See has some control over ecclesiastical goods, to an extent that varies according to the body and the goods in question, does not mean that these goods can simplistically be regarded as the property of the Holy See, any more than Government intervention in wage-bargaining means that all wages are the property of the State.

It is very often suggested that the art treasures housed in the Vatican should be sold and the proceeds distributed to the poor. Such a request is not without some basis. But Matthew 26: 6–13 and parallel texts remind us of the value of certain gestures and attitudes that others regard as wasteful. Whatever the rights and wrongs of this, such trea-sures are the fruit of the sacrifices made by whole generations, which thenceforth become the patrimony of the whole of humanity, which our generation has the duty of preserving and handing on, not of dispers-ing. Furthermore, most of the bequests were made with a 'destination clause' tying them to a particular location willed by the donor. The Vatican also houses goods belonging to individuals (the Borghese col-lection in the Vatican archives, for example). It is also debatable whether the ensemble of these art treasures really belongs to the Holy See, or whether it is rather a sort of custodian of them: Article 18 of the 1929 Treaty in fact laid down that 'the artistic and scientific treasures held in the Vatican City and the Lateran Palace' must be kept 'open to inspection by students and visitors.'

THE ECONOMIC AND FINANCIAL ADMINISTRATION OF THE HOLY SEE

Property belonging to the Holy See

It can be said without fear of contradiction that at least up to a few years ago the income and financial dealings of the Vatican were in such a complicated tangle that probably not even the pope knew what the true state was. They were in the hands of a plethora of administrative bodies, each jealously guarding its own privileges and autonomy.

While all popes since Leo XIII have tried to put some order into their affairs, Paul VI has made the most important reform in this respect: the creation, with future publication of the accounts in mind, of the Prefec-ture for the Economic Affairs of the Holy See (PAE), adjudged the 'first, and the most important, of the new offices instituted by Paul VI'; [2] it was set up by the apostolic constitution *Regimini Ecclesiae Universalis* (REU) of 15 August 1967.

The task of the Prefecture, directed by a commission of three cardinals, of which one is President (at present Cardinal Vagnozzi), and a bishop as secretary (Mgr Abbo), is to 'co-ordinate all the administrative bodies handling the property of the Holy See, and to exercise a supervisory function over them' (REU n. 117). This is spelt out in more detail in n. 120 of the constitution:

(a) To receive reports on the assets and economic state of the Holy See, consisting of accounts of income and expenditure, with provisional and final accounts for each year, from the various administrative bodies, with the exception of the special fund for the Institute for Religious Affairs; [3]
(b) To prepare overall provisional and final accounts for the Holy See for presentation to the pope; [4]
(c) To co-ordinate and oversee the most important investments and financial dealings;
(d) To examine (and then authorize) work projects, and to monitor their execution;
(e) To fix the percentage paid to the Administration of the Patrimony of the Holy See by means of a quota; [5]
(f) To audit the accounts and supporting documents of the separate administrative bodies.

By virtue of article 121 of REU, the Prefecture has the overall task of securing the sound administration of the assets of the Holy See, with the right to have recourse to the law if necessary.[6]

The control exercised by the Prefecture therefore extends over all the administrative bodies responsible for the property of the Holy See. These are:

1. *The Administration of the Patrimony of the Apostolic See* (APSA): President, Cardinal Villot; Secretary Mgr Antonetti; an *Ordinary Council* and an *Extraordinary Council*. The Ordinary Council is the successor to the old 'Administration of the goods of the Holy See,' all of whose functions it has taken over. Basically, this administers the original nucleus of goods belonging to the Holy See, those formerly belonging to the various congregations, tribunals and institutes, with the exception already noted. In particular, it is responsible for the management of all the real estate belonging to the Holy See.

A very empirical distinction is made between the assets represented by buildings housing congregations, offices, and so on, which are considered 'non-productive,' and those represented by buildings used for dwellings or any other purpose, which are considered 'productive.'

This latter category, however, has had its profitability curtailed by the thirty-year-old ban on rent increases on Italian property. Furthermore, buildings used by ecclesiastics and other dependents of the Holy See are let at reduced rents. Finally, one must remember that, with the exception of the buildings listed in Article 16 of the 1929 Treaty, the Holy See has to pay all Italian taxes, including Value Added Tax, which, in common with all other legal bodies and persons, it has to pay every ten years.

The Ordinary Council is responsible for the outlays of the Holy See: salaries for its employees, maintenance of buildings, the ordinary workings of all the bodies that make up the Roman Curia (except for the Congregation for the Missions [7]), and the administration of the palaces (except for the fabric of St Peter's [8]). It must also provide for the expenses of the College of Cardinals, the Synod of Bishops, and, at least in part, of the diocese of Rome—the Vicariate, the Lateran University, and so on.

The Extraordinary Council is the successor to the 'Special Administration of the Holy See,' which was established by Pius XI in 1929 to administer the funds provided by the Italian government in accordance with the financial provisions of the Lateran Treaty. This council therefore is responsible for virtually all the liquid assets of the Holy See (equity stock, bonds, bank deposits), but for only a very small part of the real estate income. What these liquid assets amount to is difficult to establish: if one takes the various statements made by the Holy See, the amount held in stocks and liquid cash balances would amount at present to some 120 million dollars; this valuation should be considered very much on the conservative side.

The greater part of the assets administered by the Extraordinary Council of APSA is made up of the sums made over to the Holy See by the Italian government in 1929: these sums consisted of 750 million lire in cash and one billion lire in consolidated 5% bonds, which together (bearing in mind that the consolidated bonds were at the time worth only 800 million lire) amount to some 80 million dollars at the exchange rate of the day. Since these monies were made over by the Italian government partly in compensation for expropriations suffered by the Church in various parts of Italy during the last century, Pius XI considered that in justice part should be handed over to the Italian Church—more precisely, it was destined for the construction of seminaries and parish houses in the South of the country. A further portion was invested in the building of the Palace of St Callixtus in Trastevere and the reorganization of the Vatican library and art gallery. Between 1929 and 1939 the Administration still managed the proceeds of Peter's Pence. The transfer of part of its funds to the United States just before the Second World War enabled the Holy See to save a large part of its capital. The figure given here is taken from an official statement: on 22 July 1970, when someone suggested that the amount of capital involved was between 7,000 and 8,000 billion lire, the *Osservatore Romano* commented: 'the productive capital of the Holy See, including deposits and investments, both inside and outside Italy, is far from the hundredth part of the sum suggested.' And Cardinal Vagnozzi, commenting on the sum of 300–350 billion lire suggested by Dr Massimo Spada, declared the Vatican's capital to be less than a quarter of this (*La Stampa,* 1 Apr. 1975). Remembering that one dollar was worth 19 lire in 1929, 626 in 1970 and 880 in 1977, that would make a figure of some 400 million dollars in 1975.

2. *The Government of the Vatican City State.* The administration of the Vatican City State is divided into eight departments [9] and controlled by a Commission of Cardinals, of which Cardinal Villot is President and Cardinal Guerri Vice-president.

Government expenditure is made up of staff salaries, building maintenance, provisions, and the Vatican Radio service and the museums. Income is derived from the issuing of postage stamps,[10] entrance charges to the museums,[11] minting of coins,[12] and profits on the sale of foodstuffs, clothing, tobacco and petrol within the confines of the Vatican State to certain categories of people entitled to buy them there and from the sales of the products of the papal estates at Castel Gandolfo. The government accounts balance, and are even in credit.

3. *The Sacred Congregation for the Missions (Propaganda Fide).* Unlike all the other congregations, which have had to hand the administration of their assets over to the Ordinary Council of APSA, Propaganda Fide has kept its own administration, which meets the expenses of running the congregation itself, and those of the Urbanian University and the College of Urban, from the income on the capital (real estate and title deeds in the town and the country) donated by the faithful over the centuries to the congregation itself. This too closes its accounts in balance or surplus.[13]

4. *The 'Fabbrica' of St Peter.* This organization is responsible for regulating the entry to the basilica, and for its safekeeping and maintenance; also for the archives of the basilica, the 'mosaic studio' and the excavations of the necropolis. The expenses are met from the sale of entrance tickets to the dome and the necropolis, and from the proceeds from donations made to the *'fabbrica'* itself and part of the offerings of the faithful. The accounts generally balance.

5. *The Apostolic Chamber.* In theory, this should administer all the assets of the Holy See in the event of the Apostolic See being vacant (REU n. 122). The treasurer is Cardinal Villot).

Beside these main administrative bodies, the following also have to submit their accounts to the audit of the Prefecture: the chapters of the patriarchal basilicas of St Peter,[14] St John Lateran and St Mary Major; the administrations of St Paul without the Walls, St John Lateran and St Mary Major; the Vicariate of Rome, the Lateran University, institutions for the preservation of faith (at least those not controlled through APSA); the sanctuaries of Loreto and Pompeii and the basilica of St Anthony in Padua; the Institute of Christian Archaeology, the Roman Academy of Archaeology, the Commissions of Sacred Archaeology, the House for the Relief of Suffering and associated bodies in St Giovanni Rotondo in Puglia; and other minor bodies.

The Institute for Religious Works

Founded and established by Pius XII in the Vatican City on 27 June 1942, as a successor to the Administration of Religious Works, and reorganized on 24 January 1944, the Institute for Religious Works (IOR) is responsible for 'seeing to the custody and administration of monies (in bonds and in cash) and properties transferred or entrusted to the Institute itself by fiscal or legal persons for the purposes of religious works and works of Christian piety.'

In other words, this body, of which Cardinal Villot is President of the supervisory board of cardinals, with Mgr Marcinkus President of the executive board, operates as a bank, in which organizations belonging to the Holy See, dioceses and parishes, religious orders and congregations, as well as numerous private individuals entitled to do so—employees of the Holy See, diplomats accredited to the Holy See, lay people who place at least part of their capital at the disposition of the Institute—can deposit their savings and make withdrawals when posted overseas or for other reasons. The deposits made with the Institute do not therefore belong to the Holy See, but to the fiscal and legal persons who make the deposits. This should be borne in mind when considering the investments made by the IOR, which amount to a higher figure than the liquid assets of the Holy See itself. The profit made by the bank is handed over entirely to the pope.

According to authoritative sources, the Institute has several thousand investors and holds some two billion dollars in deposits and inter-bank accounts. It has recently made some spectacular losses, particularly in relation to the Sindona affair. While APSA did not lose anything in its dealings with Sindona, and can even be said to have gained, having sold its holdings in the Property Company to him in 1969 before the shares plummetted on the Stock Exchange, the IOR lost at least the value of its holdings in the two banks involved in the crash—

Banca Unione and Finabank. But the directors of the Institute claim that their earlier gains, made through selling part of their holding in both banks, and the share options to increase its capital, made up for the later losses. Italian criticism of the IOR, as a vehicle for the flight of capital from the country at the time of the financial crisis (cf. *Populorum Progressio*, n. 24), should be modified in the light of the type of bodies and persons holding accounts, the rules governing transfer of capital within the IOR, and the world-wide scale of the operations of the Catholic Church.

Offerings collected throughout the world and redistributed by the bodies belonging to the Holy See

1. *Peter's Pence*. In the course of the last century, renewing a tradition that goes back to the eighth century in England and had long been maintained there and in other parts of Europe—Scandinavia, Poland, Hungary—Catholics throughout the world, led by the French, began sending a subvention to Rome, with the idea of helping the pope, who had then been deprived of the Papal States. This collection, called 'Peter's Pence,' is usually taken on the feast of St Peter or the preceding or following Sunday, and is aimed at helping the pope respond to the needs of the bishops throughout the universal Church. The amount involved is kept secret by the special office of the Secretariat of State responsible for administering it since 1939.[15] The pope uses these funds to defray the expenses of nunciatures and apostolic delegations, which are entitled to hold back enough to cover their costs from the amount contributed by the respective countries they serve in. But the greater part is still used for 'the pope's charity': that is, contributions—generally substantial—to 'disaster funds' set up for areas stricken by war, famine, earthquake, etc.

There is also a fund called *Elemosinaria Apostolica* (now changed to *The Assistential Service of the Holy Father* [16]) for the 'ordinary and personal' charity exercised by the pope.

2. *Pontifical Missionary Institutes and the 'Ecclesiae Sanctae' Fund*. Collections taken throughout the world on the occasion of Mission Sunday are channelled to the governing body of the Institutes, which is responsible for redistributing them in accordance with the needs of the various local Churches.[17] All the data relevant to the collection and distribution of these funds are published, in the *Attività della Santa Sede* and, in greater detail, in various specialist publications.

Each year the sum collected in the previous year is redistributed: in

1975 the sums distributed through the three Missionary Institutes amounted to a total of over 63 million dollars.[18] Reasonable estimates state that between 15% and 18% of all the aid given to the Churches of Asia, Africa and Latin America comes from these Institutes.[19] The *Ecclesiae Sanctae* fund, made up of an annually fixed quota of the amounts contributed to the Missions by every parish and diocese, seems for the moment to have an only limited success in its function of meeting special needs as they arise.[20]

3. *The Sacred Congregation for the Eastern Churches.* In the regions under the territorial jurisdiction of the Congregation for the Eastern Churches—mainly the Middle East—this body continues its task of presence and aid, by means of subsidies distributed through the eparchies for the building of churches and houses for the homeless, schools, hospitals, hospices, orphanages, for the establishment of bursaries for studies, and so on.[21]

4. *The Pontifical Commission for Latin America.* This body, in the same way, is responsible for the distribution of funds to meet the needs of the local Churches of Latin America.

5. *Pontifical Commission for the Pastoral Care of Migrants and Tourists.* This is responsible for pastoral care of emigrants and refugees, spiritual aid to nomads, and the apostolate of the sea and the air.

6. *Cor Unum.* This recently established body is intended, not to duplicate the others by distributing aid directly, but to be a co-ordinating body, organizing the Catholic Church's collaboration with the many international, national and private organizations working in the field of aid and relief.

THE ECONOMIC POLICIES OF THE HOLY SEE AND THEIR EFFECTS

The decision taken by the Holy See in recent times—since the loss of the Papal States, and more particularly since the Lateran Treaty of 1929—to live on the income from its own capital, seemed normal enough in the climate of the last century, and appeared to offer the best guarantee of its independence and autonomy from the powers and humours of the world. But in the last few years it has seriously been called into question, particularly on account of the involvement with the capitalist system it supports. So as to eliminate certain factors that most laid it open to criticism on the one hand, and in order to improve the profitability of its own investments on the other, the Holy See has laid down certain norms for its administrative bodies over the last ten years:

First, elimination of investments that could involve it in moral problems, such as pharmaceuticals, which could involve it in investing in contraceptive products; sale of all holdings in companies that either produce or could produce arms, so as not to risk compromising the Church's decisive endorsement of policies favouring disarmament and peace; sale of stocks in film companies, and so on. It has also progressively divested itself of all shares in construction companies, as it has taken an active part in the campaign against property speculation in Italy over the last few years. Its investments are now concentrated in 'utilities'—public services such as gas, electricity, telephone, and so on—and banks and insurance companies, though without neglecting some chemical, food and petroleum products.

A second norm would require the abandonment of majority stockholdings, so as to avoid any repetition of some sad experiences in the past when the Vatican representatives on company boards had to take the part of employers against trades unions, or decide licensing arrangements or processes of liquidation (as happened in the case of the *pasta* manufacturers Pantanella). This policy is also justified by the impossibility of suddenly providing extra financial resources if an enterprise in which it held a majority of the stock should run into unforeseen financial difficulties. It has chosen to spread its stockholding over a large number of companies, so that it never holds more than 1% of the equity of any.

A third criterion has been a shift from investment in Italy to other countries. It now has stockholdings and deposits in the USA, Switzerland, Germany, Japan, France, Canada, Spain and any other countries that allow free exportation of investment income. This criterion, which is certainly linked to the tendency to greater 'internationalization' of the Curia, is nevertheless dictated by economic and political considerations: investments in Italy are at present less profitable, seem less certain for the future, are less secret and more highly taxed—in some countries, the Vatican, like other religious bodies, enjoys certain tax advantages not conceded in Italy. Having got rid of most of its stockholdings in Italy, it is now proceeding to divest itself of its real estate holdings as well, either on account of the campaign against the holding of ecclesiastical property being conducted in Rome, or because of their reduced profitability.

Having made these observations, one must in all fairness state that in no case in recent years have financial considerations or economic interests been allowed to stand in the way of policy decisions. Paul VI in particular did not hesitate to put the decentralization he considered possible into practice, even though this has meant renouncing various sources of income that in the past were one reason why the Roman Curia took over so many responsibilities properly belonging to the local bishops.[22] Nor did he hold back in setting up the bodies proposed by

Vatican II, even though these involved a substantial increase in costs; [23] he incorporated local bishops as members of congregations, and called in the services of experts and consultants from all over the world, despite the difficulty of balancing the accounts with such an increase in air fares from distant parts. Finally, recent popes have seen the need for social justice to operate at the centre, and have instituted a more equitable distribution of salaries among the employees of the Holy See.[24]

This prompt implementation of the Council and progressive internationalization of the Curia, part of an overall plan to increase the relevance of Rome to the universal Church, have produced a sharp increase in expenses, just at a moment when, for various reasons, including the world economic recession, earnings have been contracting. The Ordinary Council of APSA, which is responsible for the running costs of the Roman Curia, is and has been for the last few years so much in deficit that, despite all attempts to cut costs,[25] the income of the Extraordinary Council and the Government together are not sufficient to balance the overall budget of the Holy See, which, apart from what the pope can draw from the activities of the IOR and Peter's Pence to help meet the deficit, would seem to be forced to a progressive realization of its assets.

INDICATIONS FOR THE FUTURE

Publication of the accounts

As an ecclesiology of the Church as a perfect, monarchical society gives way to an ecclesiology of communion, in the midst of which the Christian people can become conscious of being the Church, so must the assets of the Church become something public, a patrimony of the poor, subject to control by the whole community. What holds good for the assets of the local community also holds good for the Holy See.[26] It is said that Paul VI, when presented with his first set of accounts, said they were not worth publishing, as no one would believe that the Holy See could function on such a modest scale. But surely this painful realization of the low level of the estimates compared to what the Vatican is generally believed to possess should rather act as a stimulus to make its financial activities all the more accessible? The true reason for its failure to publish its accounts should rather be sought in suspicion of the civil authorities still felt and fear of expropriation, but above all in the tendency too many bodies still have to keep their income and expenditure secret, either from a power complex or from fear of being subjected to criticism, which in some cases could be severe. This last aspect leads to my next proposal.

Strengthening of the prefecture for economic affairs

The course initiated with the institution of the Prefecture for Economic Affairs, intended to provide the pope and the world episcopate with a body capable of controlling and co-ordinating the economic activities of the Vatican, should, it seems, be continued in various directions:

(a) By submitting the Prefecture itself to the regime imposed on the other departments of the Curia,[27] that is above all an extension of the principle of collegiality to it also, by setting up a 'Plenary Council,' which would co-opt diocesan bishops as members. The bishops would certainly have something to say about the progress of economic affairs and could contribute to establishing the broad lines of the economic activities of the Holy See.[28]

(b) By clarifying the rules governing the working of the Prefecture, its duties and limitations, but also the obligations imposed on other bodies in their dealings with it.

(c) By entrusting the Presidency to the Cardinal Secretary of State, and removing him from the Presidency of the bodies the Prefecture is supposed to supervise. It would appear that in the present situation control by the Prefecture is a pure formality.[29]

Containment of costs

The real solution to the problem of containing costs, which, as we have seen, the Holy See is seriously considering, lies in a radical reassessment of the services provided by the See of Peter. This should be a visible centre of communion for the universal Church, called to 'preside in charity,' a focus of spiritual and moral leadership, rather than a centralized and sacralized organizational structure. A general pruning of all the offices, many of which have become pure historical survivals or useless duplications since the recent development of the Secretariat of State; a basic reconsideration of the opportuneness and rôle of the nunciatures; a devolvement of further tasks to the diocesan bishops; greater humility in building (I am thinking of the Audience Hall, the papal terrace, the reorganization of the Museum of Modern Art); a serious rethinking of costs incurred by various artistic and scientific bodies, which are not really the direct concern of the Church and which in any case probably cannot be given the funds they need in the present situation—the Observatory, archaeological researches, certain pontifical academies; a clearer distinction between services rendered to the universal Church and those that relate to the diocese of Rome or the Italian Church: these are some proposals that can be put forward on

ecclesiological grounds, but which would certainly also show a considerable saving to the expenses of the Holy See.

Transition to financial support from the local churches

The decision taken by the Holy See to keep itself on the income from
its assets did win it a form of independence that perhaps had its uses in
the past, but today places it in a position contradictory to the official
views expressed by the papacy on economic liberalism and capitalism,
as in *Populorum Progressio*. The Vatican is financially dependent on
the capitalist system, on the profits the great multi-national corporations make out of their dealings, including those in developing countries, and therefore finds itself on the side of capitalism in certain social
conflicts. All this raises questions and doubts, particularly among the
younger Churches. Should the pope and the Holy See not now have the
greater courage required to choose poverty, and the humility to accept
a living derived from offerings and contributions that the episcopal
conferences, individual local Churches and Christians in general will
certainly not deny them? Once the wall of secrecy is knocked down,
and there is a flow of information on the real needs of this centre of
communion in the universal Church, and perhaps greater evidence that
the Roman Curia too is acting in the service of *koinonia, diakonia* and
the witness of the Church,[30] Peter's Pence might well reach the proportions of the sum donated annually for the Missions, which would then
be virtually sufficient to cover the annual costs of the Holy See. I am in
fact convinced that the Christians of today would not be less generous
than those of the young Pauline community, who so generously
supplied the needs of the mother church in Jerusalem.

Translated by Paul Burns

Notes

1. Cf. Y.-M. Congar, 'Les biens temporels de l'Eglise d'après sa tradition
théologique et canonique,' in *Eglise et Pauvreté* (Paris, 1965), pp. 234–58, with
bibliography.

2. N. del Re, *La Curia Romana* (Rome, 1970), p. 292.

3. The expression is sybilline: in fact, however, the IOS has always remained
outside the control of the Prefecture.

4. Around the end of the year, the Prefecture presents the provisional accounts of the various bodies for papal approval. In March, it presents the

overall provisional figures, called 'consolidated,' and in June the final accounts for the previous year.

5. This point has not yet been put into practice.

6. It has not yet made any intervention of this kind, both through lack of clarity and of legislative bodies.

7. To give an idea of the amounts involved in this expense, here is a list of the various bodies comprised under the term 'Roman Curia': Secretariat of State; Council for the public affairs of the Church; Congregations of the doctrine of the faith, of bishops, of the Eastern Churches, for the administering of the sacraments, of the clergy, of religious and secular institutes, for canonization causes, for Catholic education; Tribunals of the apostolic Penitentiary, of the apostolic Signature, of the Sacred Roman Rota; Secretariats for Christian unity, for non-Christians, for non-believers; the laity commission and the committee for the family; the Justice and Peace Commission, and other commissions for the revision of the Codex of the Latin Church, for the revision of the Eastern Codex, for the interpretation of the Decrees of the Second Vatican Council, for the communications media, for Latin America, for the pastoral care of emigrants and tourists; *Cor Unum;* the international theological commission, the biblical commission and eight other commissions of minor importance; offices of—the apostolic chamber, the prefecture of economic affairs, the administration of the patrimony of the Holy See, the prefecture of the apostolic house, the assistential service of the Holy Father; the archive of Vatican II; the personnel office; the central office for Church statistics.

8. The term 'Palatine Administration' includes, besides the *Fabbrica* of St Peter's: the Vatican apostolic library, the secret archive, the schools of paleography and diplomacy, the Vatican publishing house, the Vatican Polyglot Press and the *Osservatore Romano.*

9. The eight departments are: general secretariat; general administration of monuments, museums and galleries; general direction of technical services; the Vatican radio; economic services; health services; the Vatican Observatory; the pontifical villas.

10. The face value of the stamps issued in recent years (the series are sold till they are exhausted) amounted to 7,225 million lire in 1974, 3,680 million in 1975 and 6,022 million in 1976.

11. In 1976, visitors to the museums totalled 1,360,800. A ticket costs 1,000 lire, except on the last Sunday in each month, when entry is free. The museums have their own separate budget within the government, which generally balances, with the cost of custodians, restoration and maintenance of the works of art, and the laboratories attached to the museums equalling the income from the sale of tickets.

12. The currency of the Vatican City State is tied to the Italian currency; the State has the right to issue currency in limited quantities, and this is accepted throughout Italy. Besides this, there are periodic issues of commemorative series of numismatic value. For all matters relating to the minting and issuing of money and medals, see P. de Luca, *Papal Medals* (Santa Severina, 1975), predominantly numismatic in interest, but authoritative and complete.

13. A detailed description of the administrative council of this congregation

is given by the administrative delegate, Mgr Reghezza, in 'Sacra Congregazzione per l'Evangelizzazione dei Popoli,' in *Annuario* I, 1976 (Rome, 1977), pp. 120–29.

14. The chapter of St Peter's, for example, is made up of a hundred or so canons and other beneficiaries, and meets its expenses from the sale of tickets to the 'treasure' (now called the 'Historical Museum of St Peter's'), profits from some other sales and part of the offertory collection.

15. Peter's Pence reached the figure of 12–15 million dollars during the reign of John XXIII (almost the same as the amount donated to Pontifical Missionary Works), but over the last few years has decreased to some 4 million dollars annually, less than a quarter of the amount collected on Mission Sunday. Individual dioceses generally publish the amount they send to Rome as Peter's Pence.

16. The Assistential Service of the Holy Father provides the means for replying to the 5,000 special requests for help received each year, mainly from Rome and the rest of Italy; it also maintains certain ancient hospices in Rome, chiefly for girls and women 'in trouble.' The funds for this special charity are also augmented by the extremely modest tax levied on 'apostolic benedictions,' the pieces of parchment carrying the apostolic blessing handed out for weddings, ordinations, and other occasions. (In parenthesis, let it be said that this practice would be better abolished, or provided entirely free, so as to avoid the indecorous trafficking in these documents carried on by commercial practitioners around the Vatican.)

17. The funds coming into Rome are redistributed without any deduction being made for administrative expenses, so the Congregation for the Evangelization of Peoples has to finance its own running from other sources.

18. The sums collected by Propaganda Fide alone, especially on Mission Sunday, have risen from 27 million dollars in 1965 to nearly 49 million in 1975, an increase in face value which has not kept pace with inflation, so the real value has diminished. Major contributions come from the USA, Germany, Italy, Spain, France, Belgium, Holland and Australia. Propaganda Fide distributed over 50 million dollars in 1975; to this some 8 million from the Pontifical Institute of St Peter Apostle should be added (mostly spent on maintaining 46,000 seminarians in various parts of the world), and over 5 million from the Institute of the Holy Infancy (based in Paris). In 1976 the figures were just under 50 million from Propaganda Fide and 9 million from St Peter Apostle.

19. Other forms of aid are distributed directly from diocese to diocese, through the so-called 'twinning' arrangement, through missionary institutes which make their own collections, and through various bodies such as Misereor, Adveniat, Aid to the Persecuted Church, and so on.

20. This fund is named after the *motu proprio, 'Ecclesiae Sanctae,'* of 6 Oct. 1966, n. 8, produced as an application of *Ad Gentes* n. 38. Cf. 'Sacra Congregazione per l'Evangelizzazione dei popoli,' in *Annuario 1976,* I (Rome, 1977), pp. 403–7. At Easter 1977 the fund contained half a million dollars.

21. The congregation for the Eastern Churches distributed 6 million dollars in 1975 and 5,800,000 in 1976. These funds come partly from the missionary institutes, but mostly from organizations like the Catholic Near East Welfare

Association of New York, *L'Oeuvre d'Orient* of Paris, the *Catholica Unio* of Switzerland and Germany, and other special bodies in Germany and Holland.

22. Since the restitution to the bishops of faculties previously reserved to the Holy See (cf. *Pastorale munus,* 30 November 1963 and *De episcoporum muneribus,* 15 June 1966), only a few of the old taxes and benefices remain, and contributions to causes for canonization. In the case of the Roman Rota, these amount to some 20% of its overall costs, with the Holy See finding the remaining 80%.

23. The newer bodies proposed by Vatican II are the most costly: the three Secretariats, the Justice and Peace Commission, the Laity Commission, the Communications Media Commission. In fact, these bodies need far more contact at international level; their members take part in conferences all over the world, and they are lavish with their invitations and hospitality.

24. The dependents of the Holy See at the end of 1976 amounted to: 3,292 employees, 1500 retired; of these, 1391 employees and 490 retired belonged to the Government of Vatican City. Salaries are on the low side, which is a particular hardship for those who come from strong currency countries. It would seem, however, that they are among the least differentiated in the world. From a maximum of 600,000 lire per month at the peak of one's career (after ten biennial increases), budgeted in 1977 for a 'higher prelate of the first class' (e.g., the Vice Secretary of State), they descend to a minimum of 400,000, allowing for the same increases, for assistants, ushers, clerks and secretaries. The employees of the Holy See, besides the usual sickness benefits, retirement pensions and family allowances, do enjoy some special privileges: reduced rents, use of the Vatican duty-free shop, exemption from Italian tax (under art. 17 of the 1929 Treaty). The reason for the levelling out of salaries is principally that the so-called 'sliding scale,' which the Vatican applies on the Italian model, has up till now been consolidated into salaries, with a flat figure of 203,000 lire for everyone. The Cardinals' 'scale' should be considered separately: this is not a salary and does not benefit from the sliding scale, so is in need of periodic adjustment. Cardinals also lose the right to rewards for any work done in precedence over their service to the Holy See and do not benefit from health insurance. Religious, whose vow of poverty is taken into account, are treated differently; they receive 425,000 lire per month for graduates, and 400,000 for non-graduates, with no retirement pension, it being considered that their orders will take charge of this, for which they take 2½% monthly.

25. The APSA accounts for 1975 were sent back by the pope with a request for a cut in costs. The 'Gagnon commission' was set up to examine how these could be reduced, mainly through elimination of unnecessary jobs. It proposed various internal transfers and the non-replacement of persons retiring from posts considered less important, together with a curtailment of travel and invitations by the individual bodies.

26. In the *Directory on the Pastoral Office of Bishops,* published in 1973, the Holy See recommends (nn. 134–5) that diocesan and parish accounts should be published, which many dioceses and parishes throughout the world do—and did before the recommendation. It is incomprehensible that the Bishop of

Rome should not be the first to set the example and practise what he recommends others to do.

27. G. Delgado, *La Curia Romana, El Gobierno central de la Iglesia* (Pamplona, 1973), holds that the Prefecture is a body with administrative status equivalent to the Sacred Congregations (REU, 1, par. 2).

28. For many years, the Prefecture has been seeking the working method and form of control best suited to its aims: 'the Prefecture is still engaged in a better definition of its own structure and tasks' (*Attività della Santa Sede*, 1971, p. 808); 'the Prefecture is succeeding in accomplishing, though gradually, its institutional tasks . . . it has sought above all to obtain better co-operation from the administrative bodies under its control' (ibid., 1974, p. 709).

29. As we have seen, the Prefecture is presided over by Card. Vagnozzi; it has the task of supervising and controlling bodies such as APSA, whose President is the Cardinal Secretary of State (Villot), the Government of the Vatican City State, whose commission is also presided over by the same Card. Villot. It hardly needs saying that in fact these bodies can escape all control.

30. Cf. L. Sartori, G. Cereti, 'The Curia at the Service of a Renewed Papacy,' in *Concilium* 8, 1975.

Knut Walf

The Church Tax as a Means
of Subsistence

SINCE it is impossible in so short an article to give a full account of the West German church tax system with its complex ramifications and corresponding problems, I give references to the most important writing on this significant segment of German canon law, which will introduce interested readers from other local churches into an alien world.[1] And this should be emphasized from the start: what appears to the reader familiar with West German conditions 'normal' and natural must seem totally unimaginable in other local churches. In this article I will limit myself to a few aspects I regard as important, though some features of the system which I believe to be important are given little emphasis in the usual descriptions or emerge in them only indirectly.

What is the German church tax, and what is it not?

Since foreigners occasionally have wrong ideas about the German church tax, this question can be taken first. The reason for the mistaken ideas is almost certainly the unique term, off-putting as it is misleading, 'church tax.' Church tax in the Federal Republic of Germany—as far as it involves the Catholic Church—has a basis in canon law (1496 CJC) and in terms of the structures of modern economic life is a compulsory contribution in money from Church members without a specific right to any corresponding service. Article 137, paragraph 6 of the 1919 constitution of the Weimar Republic (WRV) which was adopted unaltered as Article 140 of the constitution of the Federal German Republic (the Basic Law of 1949:GG), gives religious bodies (religious associations), which are recognized by the

20

state as corporate bodies, the right 'to raise taxes . . . by means of the civil tax lists.' [2] This is where the difficulties start. It is almost impossible to explain to a foreigner, or, for that matter, to a German, in simple words what is meant by a 'corporate body.' This term, which is ambiguous, and was also much discussed in West Germany in the last two decades, is based on the very general legal concept of a union of persons. Very briefly, a corporate body is a legal concept from what is called the indirect public administration, and is usually applied to administrative entities which are to a greater or lesser degree dependent on the State. This explains the remark of the German constitutional lawyer Rudolf Smend, who, a generation ago, described the application of this term to religious bodies as a 'puzzling honorary title.' The effects of this honorary title are, however, very practical, the compulsory collection of the Church tax by an official act of the State.

Church tax does not therefore refer to voluntary donations by Church members, fees for religious services, or to the contributions for which parishes in most West German dioceses also ask Church members, or to the quite considerable direct or indirect support to the Churches from the West German State in the form of payments or privileges. According to careful estimates, these financial advantages for the two main Churches in the Federal Republic, must be of the order of thousands of millions of marks a year. Precise figures or detailed summaries are not available or are not published! In spite of the requirement of the constitution contained in Art. 138, Para. 1 WRV (= Art. 140 GG), which provides for the ending of these payments, which go back essentially to the secularization of 1803, the state annually pays stipends for bishops and cathedral chapters, supplements for the stipends of parochial clergy or funds for the maintenance of Church buildings and for new construction.[3]

How did the Church tax originate?

There is naturally evidence, even for the early period of the Church, of contributions to the Church by the faithful in money, kind or services, and in this context the mediaeval tithe is always mentioned. The roots of the particular German taxation system are, however, much more recent. The Prussian General State Code of 1794 (ALR) provided for the first time for a local rate which could be levied where church resources were inadequate.[4] This was done increasingly during the nineteenth century for various reasons (the results of secularization, the growth of the money economy, changes in the denominational structure of the population as a result of industrialization), and the system became more and more important as a means for covering Church expenditure. It must be mentioned that there were objections on the Catholic side from the hierarchy, who were unhappy about adopting the system because of the widespread practice in the non-Catholic Churches of lay participation in the administration of Church finances. The result at the end of the last century and the beginning of this was civil Church tax laws in most of the German states which were a reflection of the religious neutrality of the State. It is incorrect to treat these measures, as is sometimes done, as part of the *Kulturkampf* waged by these governments.

Generally in West Germany the Church tax is levied as a surcharge on income tax (a so-called standard tax), and varies in the different states of the Federation from 8% to 10%. Reference was made at the beginning of the article to the ramifications of the German church tax system, and a good illustration of this can be given here. It is not generally known that surcharges for the support of the Churches are included in assessments for property rates, payroll tax and wealth tax.

What are the main problems of the German system?

Let us begin our answer to this question with the aspect just mentioned. It is clear to everyone that the system of supplementary levies outlined above makes church finances almost totally dependent on state taxation policy, a fact which not only can bring the Church into a bad light and create ill-feeling but must also be open to objection from a canonical point of view, since the Catholic Church, at least, regards itself as autonomous *vis à vis* the State. In this connection, proposals are beginning to be discussed for fixing maximum rates of Church tax (the procedure known as topping), which would be based on taxable income and not on the tax rate fixed by the state. This is a move which deserves every encouragement!

A further difficulty is the inadequacy of the Church bodies responsible for the expenditure of the Church tax receipts. This affects the Catholic Church in particular, where synodal structures which give the laity a voice are still underdeveloped. In plain language this means that while all Church members have to pay tax, none of the organizations engaged in allocating the sums raised is responsible to them. In some German dioceses advisory committees on Church tax have been set up which include elected and appointed lay people with the relevant technical knowledge, but it is worth looking at the system recommended by the Fifth Special Commission of the Joint Synod of West German Dioceses. According to the commission, a Church tax committee should be made up of three officials of the diocesan administration, two parish priests elected by the council of priests and twenty laypeople not employed by the diocese. Of these twenty laypeople, three are to be appointed by the bishop and the other seventeen 'elected through parish committees.' In other words, there is no grass-roots legitimation; eight of the total of twenty-five members are directly dependent on the bishop or are people of his choosing. For the commission then to talk about 'democratic legitimation' (significantly in quotation marks!) in this context, is pure irony. Correspondingly minimal is the interest of the overwhelming majority of the payers of church tax in the use of these resources, particularly since it is only in the last few years that most German dioceses have given way to the pressure of public opinion and seen fit to make public parts of their budgets.

Another unsatisfactory, and again little-known, feature of the German system is the fees the State charges for its work. The German financial administrations take between two and five per cent—the most usual figure is four per cent—of the receipts for their services in administering the system (assessment, collection, coercive measures and deduction). Only in Bavaria is there a church tax department largely under the control of the Church (church tax offices). This means that for payers of church tax in the other Federal states the Church makes no appearance in this area at all, and the general impression given is that the church tax is a compulsory payment to the State. This naturally raises the question whether, when the psychological effects are included in the calculation, the State's help really is so cheap. It is almost certainly the marriage of convenience and interest between Church and State in this area in modern Germany which loses the Church respect among large groups of the population, the low income groups who have to count every penny and for whom topping up would bring no reduction in church tax.

It is also not widely known that because church tax is a legitimate deduction for tax purposes as a 'special payment,' the State has to accept a reduction in tax receipts running into thousands of millions of marks a year. Quite apart from this curiosity of tax law by which taxes can be set against tax in the same way as donations, it is questionable whether the State really does so well out of this system. On closer inspection, and after the stripping away of the window dressing to which many defenders of the West German system of church finance devote so much energy, so many questions are left that a fundamental reform must be considered.

How can exemption from church tax be obtained?

Let it be said at once: exemption can be obtained, but only by the extreme method of a formal declaration of intent to leave the Church as regards the civil domain. This brings me to the most sensitive feature of the German system. It should, however, be borne in mind that the internationally reputed German canonist Klaus Mörsdorf has spoken of a 'separation from the unity of the Church' with reference to so-called departure from the Church because of the church tax.[5] Mörsdorf also insists that the Church 'can use spiritual pressures (for example, exclusion from the Eucharist or interdict) to remind a recalcitrant taxpayer of his responsibility to contribute to the Church's financial needs.' [6] This illustrates sufficiently the calibre of the weapons used in this conflict. That only small numbers of people leave the Church in West Germany as compared with neighbouring western countries is clear, and, taken in isolation, is cause for satisfaction to the Church. For all the remoteness from the Church of most baptized Catholics, there are such strong ties to the Church, though with no visible rational basis, that only a disappearing and mostly intellectual minority take the step of declaring their departure from the Church before the civil courts or registrars. The motives of the majority of German Catholics who have not visited a church for years or even decades and still do not leave the Church are a complex mixture. They perhaps include the following elements: unconscious fears of a loss of identity, the desire for additional insurance (a church funeral), consideration for the feelings of the parental generation, worry about the social integration of their own children and, a considerable factor in the 'Catholic world,' fear of social control and even, still, of professional or commercial disadvantages. It is a sobering thought that this assortment of factors, which essentially amount to human weakness and immaturity, is the basis of the finances of the West German Church. To put it more shortly and more forcefully: this Church is almost 70% financed by people who, to a greater or lesser degree, no longer regard it as particularly vital. In view of such facts must we not ask ourselves, honestly, whether this system can be retained? It is ultimately a question of self-respect.

How are the receipts from the Church tax used?

This is best illustrated by the case of a German diocese which, as already mentioned, has begun in recent years to publish its budget. The budget of the diocese of Munich and Freising rose from around 241m DM in 1975 to around 299m. DM in 1977; in other words, it rose in this short comparative period by almost 25%, a much higher rate than that of general economic growth in West Germany. Comparative figures are available for the German Evangelical Church: the Evangelical Church in Wurtemberg had a budget of around 300m DM in 1977, and press estimates suggested that this would rise by a half in 1978. Comparisons of the amounts of these budgets from these local churches of the two major denominations with those of an underdeveloped country might well provide a stimulus for very practical consideration.

The figures which follow refer exclusively to the 1977 budget of Munich and Freising. 281m DM, or 94% of the total, comes from the Church tax. The contributions of the state of Bavaria amount to a mere 15m DM (5%). Only the remaining one per cent comes from the Church's own resources.

The breakdown of expenditure is as follows. 16.6m DM (5.6%) go on the diocesan administration, though of this 1.1m DM are devoted to publicity work and the training and further education of the clergy. Anyone interested in finding out the salaries of the bishops would not find the answer in these estimates. They appear—strange as this may seem to foreigners—in the government estimates.

By far the biggest item in the Munich-Freising budget is described as pastoral work: this amounts to something over 190m DM, or 63.5%. For this item in particular, one needs to take a close look at the detailed breakdown. Only 55.3m DM are spent on manpower, and a mere 10m DM on 'special pastoral expenditure,' while 125m DM, no less than two-thirds of this item, are swallowed up by the provision and maintenance of Church buildings.

Spending on schools and education is given as 17.7m DM, on extra-diocesan work as a mere 20m DM, and almost 6m DM are allocated to the reserves. Charitable and social work takes up 48.6m DM: that is, just 16.3%. It is somewhat surprising to find that this item, which people are so fond of citing to justify the Church tax system, also includes the supplementary provision for priests' housekeepers (1m DM), together with a very generous sum, 6.2m DM under the very general rubric 'unallocated resources and other.' If these two are deducted from the total, the amount left for charitable and social work is no more than 41.3m DM, or 13.8% of the budget.

In addition, the diocesan financial administration cost 7.35m DM in 1977, of which 4.4m were the costs of the church tax office, which thus accounted for 1.5% of the total budget.

What is the attitude in West Germany to the church tax?

It will be easily imagined that the situation described has given rise in West Germany to a long-standing and rather literary dispute about the church tax. Here, as in so many questions, whereas the front used to run straightforwardly between critics outside the Church and supporters who either had links with the Church or were active in it, in the last decade a wider range of views has gained ground within the Church, though critics inside it are still in a minority. Nevertheless the Joint Synod of Dioceses in West Germany has been unable to avoid discussion of the church tax, though in view of the membership of the special commission dealing with the subject one should not expect that much pain will be inflicted on the well-padded underbelly of the West German church finances. That would be rather like expecting a capitalist to argue for changing society in the direction of socialism.

This commission, Special Commission V of the Joint Synod of Dioceses in West Germany, carried out a comparison of systems of church finance throughout the world, which it presented in a working paper entitled *Tasks of the Church in State and Society* (section D, 'The Financing of the Church's Work'). Predictably, the conclusion was a eulogy of the German system. One of the main supporting arguments in this paper is the old one of the social and charitable element, which, as we have seen, cannot be accepted without challenge.

What might a defensible system of Church finance look like?

The German system undoubtedly has many elements which could be borne in mind or even adopted in a reform or in the working out of an up-to-date system of Church finance. There is, for example, no need to oppose totally in advance a limited use of the state tax-collectino man-hinery such as occurs in Bavaria. The link with the government tax-rate must, however be rejected. It is also high time a neutral institution was commissioned to undertake a cost-benefit analysis of the collaboration of Church and state in regard to church tax and government subsidies.

It is also essential to look for a defensible arrangement of the relation between financial support for the Church and active church membership. The automatic link between church membership and payment of the church tax is objectionable. Since there is no such thing as leaving the Church in canon law, the possibility of leaving the Church created by the State as part of the tax machinery is extremely inappropriate. It is also wrong for the Church to make even indirect use of legal methods which fidelity to its nature would otherwise lead it to reject most strictly.

The best thing about the German system of church finance is its roughly egalitarian character. This means independence from financially powerful individuals or groups, an aspect which is perhaps given too little attention abroad. Nevertheless the crucial advantage of this is the possibility it creates of a synodal Church, provided the other elements can be added. These are the allocation and administration of tax income by bodies deriving their authority from all church members or payers of the church tax. This criterion is a good demonstration of the glory and the shame of the system of church finance which obtains in West Germany.

Translated by Francis McDonagh

Notes

1. F. Giese, *Deutsches Kirchensteuerrecht* (Stuttgart, 1910; unchanged reissue, Amsterdam, 1965); H. Herrmann, *Ein unmoralisches Verhältnis* (Düsseldorf, 1974), pp. 133–47; C. Link, 'Kirchensteuer,' *Evangelisches Staatslexikon* (Stuttgart, 2 1975), pp. 1238–47; H. Marré, *Das kirchliche Besteuerungsrecht: Handbuch des Staatkirchenrechts der Bundesrepublik Deutschland* (West Berlin, 1975), vol. 2, pp. 5–50; J. Neumann, 'Zur Kirchenfinanzierung in der Bundesrepublik Deutschland,' in *Theol. Quartalschrift* 3 (1976), pp. 198–205.

2. H. Hildebrandt (ed.), *Die deutschen Verfassungen des 19. und 20. Jahrhunderts* (Paderborn, 1971), p. 102.

3. J. Isensee, 'Staatsleistungen an die Kirchen und Religionsgemeinschaften,' in *Handbuch des Kirchenrechts der Bundesrepublik Deutschland,* vol. 2, pp. 51–90.

4. Neumann, op. cit., p. 199, n. 3.

5. Eichmann-Mörsdorf, *Kirchenrecht,* vol. III (Paderborn, 9 1960), p. 415.

6. K. Mörsdorf, *Kirchenrecht,* vol. II (Munich, Paderborn & Vienna, 11 1967), p. 497.

William Bassett

Support of the Church
by Freewill Offering

FIFTY million Catholics in the United States support 18,527 parishes, 3894 missions and 10,074 chapels. Over eight thousand parochial elementary schools enrol 2,412,223 students; 340 private elementary schools have 66,006 students; 1601 diocesan, parochial and private high schools provide instruction for 890,062 students. There are 241 Catholic colleges and universities in the United States with 442,770 students; 387 seminaries with 11,938 students; 730 hospitals treating over 32,000,000 patients annually; 219 orphanages, 461 homes for the aged, and 116 protective institutions. Through various charities Catholics provide for the care of 31,519 dependent children. Church-related institutions employ 167,835 teachers, 107,856 of whom are laymen. The faithful in the United States support 58,301 priests, among whom 11 are cardinals, 40 archbishops, and 283 are bishops; 8745 brothers, and 130,804 religious sisters.[1] In addition, the Catholic faithful provide millions of dollars annually to the Campaign for Human Development, the Bishop's Overseas Relief Fund and to several other national and numerous diocesan special collections for charities, the support of the Holy See, and the missions.

These statistics could be expanded greatly by including data regarding other types of Catholic institutional interests such as cemeteries, ethnic, fraternal and protective organizations, and separately incorporated non-profit co-ordinating agencies such as the United States

Catholic Conference, the United States Conference of Bishops or the individual state Catholic Conferences.

OFFICIAL STATISTICS ARE INCOMPLETE

The numbers alone, however, are only a partial indication of the value of the contributions of the faithful to the Church. There are no statistics available to indicate the monetary worth of church investments in corporate securities, land, leaseholds or the immense variety of testamentary bequests received annually in diocesan and religious offices. 'There is no one person or agency, including the government, with exact knowledge of the value of church property in the United States,' observed D. H. Robertson.[2] The statement is undoubtedly correct.

It should quickly be added, however, that neither does any one person or agency know the liabilities of the Catholic Church in America. What is the cost of supporting the largest religious and charitable organization in the world? The financial administration of the Church in America is so decentralized and fragmented that no one has an answer to that question. We do know, however, that the available accumulated assets, worth perhaps $40 billion,[3] fall short of providing economic security for the personnel employed by the Church or for underwriting continuing operations.

The Catholic Church in the United States was built by the freewill contributions of the faithful. It is maintained, for the most part, in the same way. There is no doubt that the generosity of Catholics was vital when the institutions of the Church were built in the past. Similarly, there can be no hesitation in saying that the future of these institutions depends completely upon the continuing good will of the Catholic faithful. The Church in the United States is an ongoing creation of the faith of millions. There are no direct state subsidies; no private interests can be called in to sustain the cash flow if the faithful should waiver in their commitment.

The immediate corollary of this fact points to both the strength and the weakness of the Catholic Church in America. The strength of the Church is that its leadership must be exercised in a milieu of trust in the faithful for support. Correspondingly, however, church administrators must be cautious not to upset the sensitivities of those who hold the purse strings. A continuing weakness of the Catholic Church in America is a preoccupation with the desires and expectations of the monied contributors, the stalwarts of parish and diocesan fund drives. Catholics in the United States are overburdened with administrative and institutional concerns. There are too many shepherds. Prophets, social critics, and mystics are rare among the clergy. The routine of the parishes, dioceses and religious institutions frequently stifles the witness of a truly prophetic detachment.

A LAW OF THE CHURCH

In 1791 the first synod of the Catholic Church in the United States decreed that the clergy should be supported in accordance with the ancient custom of Christians by means of the voluntary offerings of the faithful. The offerings were to be divided into three parts, one of which was applied to the maintenance of the Church, a second for the poor, and a third for the support of priests.[4]

Statute VII of the Synod ordered priests to admonish the people at the time of mass of their duty to support the Church. It further decreed that in every congregation persons should be appointed to collect the offerings of the faithful. Statute XXIII ended the Synod with a warning to the faithful that those who did not support the clergy were violating divine law and would be answerable to God. Those who failed to support the Church, the Synod concluded, were to be held unworthy of absolution for depriving the poor of opportunities both spiritual and temporal.[5]

Six months after the closing of the Synod, Bishop John Carroll issued the first of many pastoral letters from bishops calling the laity to the financial support of the Church. Synodal and conciliar legislation for Catholics in the United States repeated these decrees and admonitions.[6] Diocesan statutes continued the law as new bishoprics were created throughout the country. The famous *Baltimore Catechism,* which was used throughout the United States until well into the twentieth century, and is still used today in many conservative parishes, raised American synodal legislation to the rank of a constitutional law of the Church universal. No Catholic could escape the obligation or plead ignorance of its burden. The support of the Church was regularized in the nineteenth century along three different lines: pew rent, tithing and offertory collections. The latter two prevail today, with offertory collections at mass systematized through a regular parish accounting system by the use of weekly envelopes. The envelope system, a creation of the 1920s, is the modern pastor's practical aid for keeping financial tab on his sheep.

THE RISE FROM POVERTY

The Catholic Church in America in the nineteenth century was desperately poor. Immigrants flooded the cities by the thousands, far outstripping any resources the Church could muster. Attacks by American Nativists, Know-nothings and a variety of other bigots set the hierarchy upon a determined course to build schools, organize protective institutions and provide the faithful with every kind of institutional insulation from the dangers to the faith. Money for this was sought in Europe. The Society for the Propagation of the Faith in France, the Leopoldinen-Stiftung of Vienna, the Ludwig-Missionsverein of Bavaria and many other charitable organizations were founded to raise money for the Church in America. Financial support came directly or was sent through the Congregation of the Propaganda Fide in Rome. This aid continued until after the First World War, when the Catholic Church in the United States finally achieved financial independence from Europe.[7] The second and third generation of immigrants assimilated into American life brought the Church relative prosperity and the institutional consolidation that undergirded the enormous building boom of the pre-Vatican II era.

PROBLEMS WITHIN THE FINANCIAL ADMINISTRATION
OF THE AMERICAN CHURCH

Since Vatican II, the Catholic Church in the United States has engaged in a probing re-examination of its entire institutional mode of operation. A short delineation of the major operational problems to surface may be helpful, if for no other reason than to point out the difficulty of trying to find solutions to them within the principles and institutes of the existing canon law.

The rich and the poor

There are bound to be great economic disparities between parishes, dioceses and among the clergy in a system as decentralized administratively as the Catholic Church in America. To overcome the inevitable inequities the dioceses have attempted several methods of equalization. Almost all diocesan statutes now set a standard remuneration for the clergy, providing from diocesan assets funds to augment the salaries of the clergy serving poorer parishes. Several bishops have also developed systems of centralized buying to save money for individual parishes and schools by purchasing supplies at bulk prices.

Among the parishes themselves, however, attempts at equalization and interparochial cooperation have met with uneven success. Only one diocese, LaFayette, Louisiana, has completely centralized in the chancery accounts all income and disbursements from the parishes.

Most dioceses encourage the richer parishes to send surplus funds to the chanceries for dispersal to others as low-interest loans. Some larger dioceses have tried to pair inner-city and suburban parishes for their mutual assistance. Direct subsidization by the dioceses to poorer parishes is, of course, very common.

The principal obstacle to interparochial financial sharing, however, is an offshoot of the canonical notion of the parish as a benefice of the clergy.[8] All efforts at co-operation must be voluntary, and thus ultimately subject to frustration by a recalcitrant pastor standing on his prerogatives.

On a national level the Catholic Church Extension Society, a private charitable organization based in Chicago, provides great assistance to poor dioceses and missions. Bishops individually may also directly assist other bishops in financial difficulties in informal ways. Yet there remains no official way in which diocesan funds can be used to help other dioceses. Any cash flow of an official nature out of the dioceses is directed towards Rome, either directly or through the Apostolic Delegation.

The place of the laity

Parish councils are rapidly providing lay assistance to parish operations everywhere. The councils have not replaced, but tend to complement the rôle of pastorally-appointed parish trustees. In canon law, however, the pastor remains ultimately responsible for the financial condition of the parish.[9] The rôle of the laity is consultative and executive.

On a diocesan level there are relatively few pastoral councils with strong lay participation in America. Even where these councils are in operation, the diocesan counsultors, an exclusively clerical body, have the final consultative vote with the bishop.

In twenty-one states the dioceses are civically incorporated as a corporation sole, with all authority over property and finances in the bishop. In the other states several kinds of trustee corporation are used. The trustees, however, in the civil charters of incorporation are all clerics. Nowhere in the United States do the laity have a legal right to a voice in the financial administration of the dioceses. No attempt has been made to amend diocesan civil incorporation papers to reflect Vatican II's change in the theological status of the laity. It is not unfair to report that the integration of the laity into the financial structures of the church remains largely a token.

Disclosing the accounts

Shortly after the close of the Vatican Council Cardinal Ritter of St Louis became the first prominent American bishop to publish a financial statement of the diocesan accounts. Since then some bishops have followed this lead. Yet in the majority of dioceses only the bishop, the vicar general or chancellor and the consultors know the condition of the diocesan books. There is, of course, no obligation in canon law to disclose the accounts to the laity.[10]

On a parish level annual statements are becoming common, although there are no standardized forms and very little assistance is given to parishioners in understanding the figures with their respective itemization.

No disclosure of the accounts of the Bishops' Conference, the Apostolic Delegation, or even the Catholic Near East Society or the Society for the Propagation of the Faith has ever been made to the laity.

The old and the infirm

Provisions for the old and the infirm among clergy and religious are very uneven. The Council promised priests and religious that their earthly cares would be met by post-conciliar reforms. The Synod of Bishops in 1971 reiterated the promise. Absolutely nothing has been done to improve the lot of priests or religious by Rome or by the national conference of bishops.

In the early 1960s the federal government gave the clergy and religious in America the option of joining the national social security programme. No one knows how many actually joined. With the advent of post-Vatican II mandatory retirement provisions, the dioceses began to provide their own group health insurance and pension plans, with costs shared by the parishes, the diocese and the individual priests and religious.[11]

In 1970 the National Federation of Priests' Councils undertook an analysis of the diocesan plans. The conclusion of a careful study was that the diocesan plans are largely underfunded, uneven in their benefits and ultimately unreliable. In their place the NFPC proposed a national health and pension plan for all employees of the Church in America to be underwritten by one or several of the major private insurance companies. The American bishops to date have refused even to consider the feasibility of this plan.

The canon law requires the individual bishop or religious superior to care for his own. There is no canonical requirement that the Church in America should take care of its own.

Disposing of obsolete institutions

Technically the assets of the Church are the patrimony of the poor, as elsewhere discussed in this volume. In practical terms this means that surplus income should go to the poor [12] and that the poor should have a favoured place in the charitable and social mission of the Christian people. It does not mean that the poor can claim the capital assets of the Church.

The canons governing the alienation or selling of church goods and properties contain three obstacles to the invasion of capital that are fairly insurmountable. First, no administrator can make a gift, sale or exchange of church property except for an urgent need. Urgent need is defined in the canons as a need *of the Church*. [13] Second, money received by way of alienation must be invested, carefully, safely and usefully in favour of the Church. [14] It cannot be spent. Third, the permission of the Holy See must be obtained to sell, give, pledge, mortgage, or lease church property or contract debts of a major sum. [15] This means that administrators of church property can give small alms and moderate gifts only.

Several years ago a well-known archbishop made the national headlines with a grand offer to sell an empty and unused inner-city parish to raise funds for the poor. He changed his mind quickly after receiving a call from the Apostolic Delegate. The plan, of course, was impossible in canon law. If there was to be a sale, it would have to have the approval of Rome. That approval would come only with the condition that the proceeds be invested for the Church, not the poor.

No responsible person wants to give up prudent safeguards to protect the property of the Church against loss by foolish zealots. On the other hand, persistent involvement of Rome in the internal financial affairs of the American Church is unnecessary either from a theological or a prudential point of view. Roman interference rarely provides help or a solution to the problem of disposing equitably of obsolete and unused institutions. It is part of the problem.

INDIRECT GOVERNMENTAL SUBSIDIZATION

The First Amendment to the federal Constitution prohibits any governmental establishment of religion or prohibition of its free exercise. Direct support of a particular Church or even of religion in general by the State is unconstitutional. Though the State must be religiously neutral, there are a number of state and federal educational and welfare programmes that indirectly aid religion. Two areas of indirect assistance are hotly debated today in the United States. Opinion as to constitutional legality is divided.

Church property tax exemption and tax incentives

Real and personal church properties devoted directly to religion are exempt from taxation. This is true of property taxes as well as income taxes. One reason for the exemption is that the churches are thought to fulfil a valid secular function in society. An equally convincing reason, derived from the leading Supreme Court case to uphold the constitutionality of the exemption, *Walz v. Tax Commission*,[16] is that taxation would involve an excessive entanglement of the State in religion, because of the need for continued evaluations of religious assets, thereby jeopardizing the free exercise clause.

In fact, the exemption of churches from taxation amounts to an indirect federal and state grant in aid. Other taxpayers must absorb an increasing amount of the tax burden for governmental services, whereas the Church receives these services free.

Contributions to religion are considered contributions to charity and thus are also tax-deductible.[17] This, of course, provides a great incentive to individual contributors to give money to the churches. The deductibility of religious contributions from gross taxable income matches also exemption from gift taxation of certain kinds of gifts and bequests to the Church. The result of these two incentives gives the churches an unparalleled advantage in raising money. State tax laws generally follow the federal internal revenue code.

The removal of tax exemptions and incentives from federal and state revenue codes would be an institutional disaster for the Catholic Church in America.

Federal and state aid to church organizations

Incredible as it may seem, the number and diversity of federal and state programmes that provide aid to church organizations in America are so great that no one knows the exact dollar amount of indirect governmental subsidization of religion. There are, for instance, more than 250 federal aid-to-education programmes alone, and Catholic parochial schools are participating in most of them. An estimated total of $5.5 million in federal church-grants may be conservative, to which another $1 billion given to churches by state and municipal authorities must be added.[18]

The principal sources of federal aid are the Hill-Burton Act, the

National Defence Education Act of 1958 (often renewed and expanded), the Higher Education Facilities Act of 1963, the Economic Opportunity Act of 1964, and the Elementary and Secondary Education Act of 1965. In addition, however, churches cut in on many other federal-aid benefactions.[19] The rationale for this enormous cash flow is that the government is merely hiring the churches to perform welfare services more cheaply than could be done in any other way. The aid to religion is indirect. Yet there is no doubt that federal subsidization enlarges the tax-exempt ecclesiastical structure and frees church assets to be used in other areas. By far the principal benefactors of federal aid are Catholic institutions.

The five programmes of the Hill-Burton Act, originally passed in 1946, have been expanded increasingly to provide most of the construction funds for all hospitals in America. There is hardly a city in America in which a large Catholic hospital has not been built with federal Hill-Burton funds. A fair estimate of $50 million per year for Catholic hospital construction and expansion is not exaggerated. To this one must add the fact that most of the elderly and practically all disabled persons pay for their care through federal Medicare, social security or other plans. Most others pay through private health insurance programs.

Under the Higher Education Facilities Act of 1964 Catholic colleges and universities have greatly expanded their dormitory, classroom, library and auxiliary facilities. Together with federally insured student loans and other forms of student aid, the total amount of subsidization may reach annually a half a billion dollars. Free meals and health services and many other smaller programmes could be added. Catholic hospitals and Catholic higher education in America are almost completely dependent now on federal monies. It is only on the level of elementary and secondary education that Catholic church schools do not receive decisively significant aid.[20]

In half the states, the transportation bill for church schools is paid by the taxpayers. In others, textbooks provided by the state for public schools are also made available for parochial schools. The Supreme Court has decided that state bond issues to build buildings on sectarian campuses are constitutional.[21]

The unmistakable result of the largely post-World War II federal and state programmes that have poured money into church institutions in America is not only that the programmes bring increasing state control over church institutions; it is also that the leadership of the Church has already commenced to look more to government and less to the faithful for financial support for these institutions. This is true particularly on levels above that of the parish. Catholics generally are not aware of the degree of dependence the Church has on the State. The myth of self-sufficiency prevails while continued lobbying efforts are being made to obtain more tax money to aid the schools in voucher plans, tax deductions for tuition plans, and other proposals.

CONCLUSION

This brief sketch of the financial structures of the Catholic Church in America has deliberately bypassed use of the typically canonical forms of taxation and fees within the Church itself, such as the *cathedraticum,* stole fees and stipends, dispensation fees and administrative expenses levied for tribunal services. I have avoided the obvious existence of tuition for educational institutions, insurance plans for hospitals, and a panoply of other devices, such as parish socials, lotteries and bingo games. Whereas the amount of money raised in these ways is considerable, in my judgment the truly serious, long-term problems the Church must face do not lie here. Major problems lie rather in the two areas discussed: namely, in the direct freewill support by the faithful and the indirect support of the government. Both a failure of trust within the Church itself and an unreflective dependence by the hierarchy upon the State could ultimately spell great trouble for the Catholic Church in the United States. At the present juncture, therefore, nothing short of absolute candour must be required of administrators of the Church.

Notes

1. *The Official Catholic Directory,* Part III, Statistical Resume (New York, 1977).
2. *Should Churches Be Taxed?* (New York, 1968), p. 17.
3. James Gollin, *Worldly Goods* (New York, 1971), p. 285.
4. 1791 Synod, Statutes V, VI, VII. *Collectio Lacensis,* Vol. III (Friburgi-Brisgoviae, 1870–1892), p. 3.
5. In 1884 the Third Council of Baltimore forbade priests to deny absolution to persons found wanting in this respect. *Acta et Decreta Concilii Plenarii Baltimorensis Tertii* (Baltimore, 1886), n. 272. The refusal of Confirmation, Marriage and Christian Burial to those not supporting the church continued, however, and even occurs in some parishes today.
6. III Provincial Council of Baltimore (1837), *Collectio Lacensis,* Vol. III, p. 56; IV Provincial Council of Baltimore (1840), ibid., p. 71; I Plenary Council of Baltimore (1852), ibid., p. 145; II Plenary Council of Baltimore (1866), ibid., p. 431; III Plenary Council of Baltimore (1884), ibid., decr. 273, p. 586.

7. On the support of the American church by European Catholics, see Theodore Roemer, *Ten Decades of Alms* (St Louis, 1942).

8. Canon 463, with Canon 1507 (CIC).

9. Canon 470 (CIC).

10. The only obligation in canon law to make an accounting respects disclosure by inferior church administrators to superiors. There is no duty of a superior to disclose his books to those beneath him in the hierarchical structure. Cf. Canons 340, 535, 1492, 1521, 1529 (CIC).

11. In 1967 the Apostolic Delegation in the United States forwarded to all ordinaries detailed provisions for the retirement of residential bishops. Among these provisions, for which the diocese is responsible, are not only a home, car, housekeeping and secretarial services, but a very generous retirement income. The contrast between retirement benefits that the bishops have provided for themselves and those of the clergy and religious is striking. The episcopal retirement plan has not been published.

12. Canon 1473 (CIC).

13. Canon 1530 (CIC).

14. Canon 1531 §3 (CIC).

15. Canon 1532 §1 (CIC).

16. 397 U.S. 664 (1970).

17. Internal Revenue Code, §§ 501–514.

18. Robert T. Miller, 'Notes on Church-State Affairs,' in *The Journal of Church and State,* Vol. 9, p. 427 (1967).

19. E.g., long-term low interest loans under Housing and Urban Development programmes, acquisition of Surplus Government Commodities and Property, Research and Development Grants from the National Science Foundation, and so on.

20. Patrick S. Duffy, 'A Review of Supreme Court Decisions, On Aid to Nonpublic Elementary and Secondary Education,' *The Hastings Law Journal,* Vol. 23, p. 966 (1972).

21. *Hunt v. McNair,* 413 U.S. 734 (1973).

Frederick R. McManus

Solicitation of Funds and Accountability

THE PAST decade has seen, at least in the United States, vastly increased awareness of responsibility, and consequent accountability, in the use of church funds—whether for the poor, for the ministers of the Church, or for the institutional Church itself. A significant dimension of this, again in the United States, is the troublesome question of solicitation of funds. The purpose of this brief article is to report on a particular development, namely, formal guidelines for alms seeking adopted by the American conference of bishops and by the conferences of superiors of religious institutes.

In an oversimplified fashion, the question is sometimes thought to affect only alms seeking by religious, and the matter was rather neatly resolved by the 1917 code of canon law in favour of the authority of the local ordinary with regard to collections taken up in the diocese, even though this had to be qualified by the privileges of mendicants and other religious. The problem, however, is equally present in the solicitation of funds within the local church by the bishop himself or by those who in some way seek support for all manner of church-sponsored charitable, educational, and health institutions. Still more important, the problem has been magnified many times over by the potential of mass mailings across diocesan lines, often with the employment of computerized mailing lists, or the use of television and radio, the style and mentality of contemporary publicity and advertising turned to church use, in fact the development of communications in a culture far different from that in which the sources of the modern canons were conceived.

Certainly, the present general law of the Church has been inadequate in the face of these developments to provide much more than the broadest indications of principle: that the local Church should have some interest in the genuineness of the solicitation of funds, that the intentions of the donors should be scrupulously respected, that such funds should be prudently and wisely administered for the good of the poor of the Church, and the like. To this may be added something hardly thought of in the sacred canons of the past, that even the appearance of excessive church wealth has to be avoided if indeed the Church is a pilgrim Church living in the last times, the Church of the poor.

In the face of all this, the canons are inadequate and it is unlikely, in the framework of universal legislation, that a revision of canons will resolve the problems. These doubtless differ from country to country. Again to give an example from the United States, there is considerable discussion about the legitimate proportion of collected funds which may be expended for fund-raising administration and costs themselves. This issue is applicable in our society to charitable and educational institutions, including local churches and religious institutes, which are recognized juridically by the individual states of the federal Republic and accorded the civil concession of freedom from taxation.

In past generations mishandling of funds and inappropriate styles of alms seeking have occurred. More often than not, however, these matters were not publicly discussed and the issue of accountability to the Christian community was rarely urged. Fortunately, we live in a period of change not only in ecclesial structures but also of ecclesiological attitudes, and the solicitation of funds—and the subsequent use of those funds—will surely be subject to scrutiny by the Christian community.

In the United States the problem has been exacerbated by several instances of unwise use of funds solicited and, in fewer cases, of notorious abuses. These form the setting in which the National Conference of Catholic Bishops, the Leadership Conference of Women Religious, and the Conference of Major Superiors of Men adopted in 1977 the guidelines which form the substance of this report.

It is unnecessary to describe in detail, especially by designating individuals or institutes, the actual problem cases. But several examples should be mentioned.

First, any number of dioceses, parishes, missions, and religious institutes engage in mail and even radio and television solicitation of funds.

Generally this is on a limited scale with mailing lists easily available. At times, however, it becomes a solicitation of massive proportions, one institute being reported as sending close to a million requests for funds in a highly computerized operation. In the case in question, there is no indication of mishandling or misappropriation of funds. The will of the donors has evidently been respected, even though critics might say that disproportionate sums are expended on the building of institutions rather than on more direct charitable, educational, or missionary purposes.

A current notorious case involves allegations concerning a retired diocesan priest who, with the best intentions but without formal or sufficient official authorization, collected funds for missionary purposes in a foreign diocese. There is evidence that such funds were indeed transmitted to the bishop of that local church, but the complete lack of accountability has been seriously challenged in the Catholic and public press.

One highly publicized fund-raising venture of a religious institute, largely the work of a single priest now under civil indictment, involved a whole series of apparent abuses: the use of improper techniques which appealed more to the greed of the donors than to their charity; a pattern of costly mailings completely out of proportion to the donations received; use of the funds in investment, loans to political figures, and holdings quite out of keeping with the corporate poverty of a religious institute; and the minute proportion of the funds expended for the purported religious and missionary purposes.

Another case, this time without allegations of any wrong-doing whatever, involved a charitable institution for boys and young men, which had been unusually successful in its Catholic and Christian programme and also in its fund-raising endeavours. After public criticism that the endowment and its income had grown to proportions which were no longer necessary for the actual operation or future of the institution itself, the latter moved to employ its surplus funds in three major research centres, two of them quite distinct and autonomous, where basic and applied research is carried on in fields closely related to the charitable purposes of the institution itself—and thus presumably of the donors.

Finally, there have been the instances in the United States of both dioceses and religious institutes close to bankruptcy, as civilly incorporated entities, because of naive or inept management of funds, reliance upon speculators, and the like. These, of course, are examples of poor administration and lack of responsible accountability rather than of the problems connected with the actual solicitation of funds for church purposes. But they are an important part of the climate in which the guidelines on fund-raising by agencies of the local church or religious institutes in the United States were drawn up.

In November 1977 the National Conference of Catholic Bishops formally approved the guidelines which will be described below. They had already been approved, in the light of 'a mutual concern that Christian motivation be expressed in all fund-raising efforts of the Catholic Church,' by the Leadership Conference of Women Religious (the canonical association of Major superiors) and the Conference of Major Superiors of Men. The best service that can be performed by this paper is to summarize the document itself, with extensive quotation. It is entitled 'Principles and Guidelines for Fund-raising in the United States by Arch-dioceses, Arch-diocesan Agencies and Religious Institutes.' (The complete text has been published in pamphlet form by the Publications Office of the United States Catholic Conference in Washington.)

STEWARDSHIP

The first section of the document is concerned with the religious motivation both of the church body which seeks funds and of the recipients. This is treated under the heading of Christian stewardship, in terms which have been common enough among non-Catholic Christians but which have been articulated in Catholic circles only during recent years. The point of the guidelines under this heading, which like other parts of the document are quite simple and straightforward, begins: 'Christian stewardship is the practical realization that everything we have is a gift from God. Stewardship expresses itself as an integral force in Christian life by motivating us to share our goods with others.' With this foundation and a brief explanation of its implications, the following guidelines are given:

1. The fund-raising appeal should be directed toward motivating the faithful to participate in apostolic works in fulfilment of their responsibility to share with others.
2. No organization should ask the faithful to fund its total and absolute security. Nor should an organization engage in fund-raising efforts for undefined future needs.
3. The trust relationship between donor and fund-raiser requires that funds collected should be used for the intended purpose and not be absorbed by excessive fund-raising costs.
4. Appeals for funds must be straightforward and honest, respectful, and based on sound theological principles. The donor must

be informed how the donated funds will be used and assured that the funds given are used for the purpose intended and that restrictions stated by the donor will be observed.

Again, like most of the specific agreed guidelines, these need little explanation. The reference in no. 3 to funds not being 'absorbed by excessive fund-raising costs' refers to the issue already mentioned, which is common to fund-raising efforts for charitable purposes in the United States: the danger that large proportions of the contributions will go to administrative costs, salaries of fund-raisers and staffs, costly techniques of public relations and publicity, and so on. As is rather obvious, no. 2 of the guidelines serves to remind both local churches and religious institutes that absolute security, which might possibly be achieved by total endowment, is hardly appropriate for the Church of the poor which lives with faith in the Lord.

RELIGIOUS AUTHORITY

A somewhat more complex matter is the formal approbation of fund-raising efforts under Catholic auspices, which clearly employ the name of 'Catholic.' The principle at stake and the reason for the guidelines are summarized by stating that the ecclesiastical authorization 'must be clear and explicit because the Church's integrity relies upon that authority [of the Church] as responsible for the method and scope of fund-raising, for the faithful disposition of the monies collected, and for the prevention of abuses.' Questions do arise, and are not entirely resolved by the American guidelines, when dealing with the question of 'public' solicitation or subscription. The reference under this heading to 'the collection of funds by public subscription' is accompanied by the following puzzling note:

See Apostolic Letter *Ecclesiae Sanctae,* August 6, 1966, No. 27 (2). Some Canonists regard 'public' subscription as an appeal for donors to contribute toward a stated purpose on the implied condition that others will contribute to the same cause. The appeal is 'public' not because it may be directed to a widespread audience, as are some mail campaigns, but because of attendant circumstances, such as endorsements by church and civil officials, with notable publicity.

Needless to say, it is difficult to establish precise guidelines when it is so easy in present day circumstances to solicit funds across the boundaries of the local churches. Entirely apart from the question of fund-raising by religious agencies, serious concern is being expressed in the United States today over the invasion of privacy by widespread telephone solicitation for funds, vast mailings of unwanted literature, including fund-raising appeals, and the like. In any event, the following are the formal guidelines proposed under the heading of religious authority:

1. Religious institutes and diocesan agencies should observe those prescriptions of canon law and their own regulations which require approval of major superiors and/or the ordinary of the place to solicit funds.
2. The approval of fund-raising by proper authority should express the purpose for which the funds are raised and the methods to be used in raising them. Effective control of fund-raising programmes should be maintained through periodic review and, where necessary, appropriate sanction.
3. Religious or diocesan agencies may not proceed in the collection of funds by public subscription without the consent of the ordinaries of those places where the funds are collected.
4. Major superiors of religious institutes should, as a moral duty, provide the ordinary of the place where the fund-raising originates with significant information about the fund-raising programs and the apostolates they support.

The fourth of the above guidelines, it may be noted, appears to refer directly to the problems created in one of the cases mentioned at the beginning of this article. In the case in question, the local church was considerably embarrassed by the discovery of fund-raising methods which had been carried on, without reference to the local bishop, by a religious institute with provincial headquarters in the diocese.

ACCOUNTABILITY

Although the canon law makes provision for accountability to ecclesiastical superiors in the administration of church funds, the guidelines agreed upon in the United States go far beyond this kind of responsible accounting. For one thing, they enforce the basic principle that the intentions of the donor must be scrupulously respected and therefore demand that reports and other information be made available to donors. Moreover, the guidelines reflect new ecclesial insights in asking for public accountability. This is a recognition of the trust which the whole church community (and civil society as well) places in the dioceses and religious institutes; more important, it is a reminder that accountability within the community of believers is not satisfied merely by reporting to hierarchical authority but entails responsibility to the Christian people.

1. Accountability requires the fund-raiser to provide timely reports on the extent to which promises expressed or implied in the solicitation of funds have been fulfilled.
2. Fund-raising reports should be prepared in scope and design to meet the particular concerns of those to whom reports are due: namely, the governing body and membership of the fund-raising organization itself, religious authorities who approved and must monitor the fund-raising effort, donors to the particular organization and the giving public at large, and those who are beneficiaries of the funds given.
3. Fund-raising reports should provide both financial information and a review of the apostolic work for which the funds were raised. The availability of these reports to benefactors on a regular basis or on reasonable request should be publicized.
4. Fund-raising organizations should provide their governing bodies with an annual audit prepared in accordance with generally accepted accounting principles.
5. All financial reports of a fund-raiser should be consistent with the annual audit. At minimum, a fund-raiser's report, regardless of scope, should set forth the amount of money collected, the cost of conducting the fund-raising effort, and the amount and use of the funds disbursed.
6. Donations should be acknowledged with promptness; reasonable requests from donors for information about their particular gift should be met.

The intent and meaning of the above guidelines are obvious enough. Perhaps one note should be added: it has long been the practice in a majority of American parishes and appears now to be the practice in a majority of parishes, and dioceses as well, that annual reports of financial matters should be made to the Catholic community. The guidelines on accountability acknowledge this as a particular responsibility in the case of solicitation of funds by dioceses and religious institutes for their respective purposes.

TECHNIQUE

The methods of contemporary advertising and publicity have grown into a highly developed art, sometimes innocent and respectable.

Techniques which appeal to proper motivation are entirely applicable to fund-raising for religious purposes. Matters of taste and judgment aside, some techniques are on the contrary shoddy and unworthy. In principle, 'responsible and effective fund-raising methodology should never drown out the voice of the Spirit of God that must permeate our total efforts.' On this basis, a series of guidelines was developed:

1. Funds beyond operating expenses should not be accumulated by a fund-raising office, but should be turned over at regular intervals to the appropriate allocating office of the organization.
2. Fund-raising authority and investment authority should not be vested in any single person.
3. Special care should be taken to see that ethical business relationships are maintained by fund-raisers with suppliers of goods and services.
4. Contracts between a religious fund-raiser and commercial suppliers and consultants should insure that control over materials, designs, money and general operations remain fully in the hands of the religious fund-raiser.
5. In no case should agreement be made which directly or indirectly base payment either to the commercial firm or to the religious fund-raiser on a percentage basis.
6. Requests for funds should not be associated with material objects which are inconsistent with the apostolic purposes of the appeal.

A couple of the guidelines require explanation. The second rule—division of fund-raising authority and investment authority—has reference to the problem created when nearly absolute responsibility is reposed in an individual person or an individual staff; the distinction and differentiation of functions can be a safeguard against abuse.

The fourth and fifth of the guidelines under the heading of techniques refer to the common practice of dioceses, religious institutes, parishes, and other bodies to employ the services of commercial firms and experts in the field of fund-raising. It is easy enough for the religious body or organization to lose control of the whole process; it is a serious abuse when, as has occurred, a percentage of the funds raised (rather than a predetermined fee or charge) accrues to the fund-raising firm or individual.

The sets of guidelines which have been quoted and commented on above conclude with some directions for local ordinaries and major superiors to implement their agreed statement, in particular to exercise genuine control and to investigate alleged abuses, to promulgate the guidelines, and to continue the cooperation of the National Conference of Catholic Bishops, the Leadership Conference of Women Religious, and the Conference of Major Superiors of Men in this field.

One final observation may be made. There seems to have been, in the preparation of these guidelines, particularly good sense in expressing them broadly and reasonably without resorting to the formalities of legislative enactments. Each of the sets of guidelines is preceded by an explanation which appeals to the highest motives of those who engage in the solicitation of funds for the poor and for the apostolic causes of the local churches and the religious institutes. While experience will doubtless reveal other problems which have to be resolved in this area and may even demand somewhat more specific requirements, perhaps the best feature of the document that has been reviewed is its Christian tone and attitude toward stewardship of God's gifts.

Paul M. Boyle

The Religious Congregation

THE financial condition of religious congregations traditionally was kept so secret that most religious were totally uninformed about their own economic situation. In many communities even today a financial report is not shown to the ordinary members. As a result, the large real estate holdings of the religious orders induce many religious and lay persons to suspect that there is great wealth in the religious congregations.

There is neither great wealth, however, nor great abuse of funds within religious communities. While only public accountability will dispel the illusion of the one or the other, perhaps this article may shed some light on the secrecy. Although these comments are applicable to most religious institutes, the focus is on an international religious order with provinces in a number of different countries. This article will discuss the needs, sources, management, and disbursement of funds within a religious congregation.

EXTERNAL NEEDS

Religious congregations are missionary by their nature. They are engaged in a wide variety of apostolic services, each of which costs money. As an integral part of its mission to serve, a religious order is obliged to search for and carefully administer the necessary funds. A few health and educational ministries are self-supporting, but most apostolic services require financial assistance from the sponsoring religious community. Religious often engage in various fund-raising activities to support these apostolates, in addition to receiving donations and bequests from generous benefactors. It is a rare apostolic service which is not dependent in substantial part on such benefactions.

INTERNAL COMMUNITY NEEDS

On the economic level as well as on the relational level a religious congregation resembles a family. Not all in the religious family are breadwinners. The contribution of the non-income-producing members is, nevertheless, essential and sometimes constitutes one of the primary purposes for the existence of the congregation. Approximately 40% of the membership of a religious congregation are in this category: about 20% devoted to internal community service and administration; 10% sick or retired; 5% in initial formation and graduate studies; 5% gratuitous ministries. These religious receive no salary or stipend, although in some countries social security or pension programmes may provide partial relief for the elderly and sick. Care of sick or retired religious, plus education and formation of new candidates, requires twice the amount needed to support other religious. The remaining 60% of the religious family must provide enough income to support their fellow religious.

Private studies by religious congregations in America suggest that it costs approximately $3,500 annually to maintain an average religious (including room, board, personal care, religious and professional responsibilites). Estimates by treasurers from several countries suggest that this figure may represent the situation in a number of western nations. If $3,500 is a reasonable average for the annual support of a religious in America half a billion dollars are needed to support 165,000 religious. This sum prescinds completely from the expenses for their apostolic activities. For some religious and in some communities the expenses can be considerably higher.

It is impossible to estimate the amount of money earned or collected annually by religious, even within one country. But a few simple figures may help us gain some appreciation of the sums involved. If we consider the wide variety of developmental sustaining and evangelical services performed by missionaries in third world countries (farms, schools, hospitals, orphanages, retreat centres, parishes, and so on) it seems safe to suppose that all of this costs at least ten dollars a day for each missionary. A sister, for example, operating a small school for one hundred children, would have expenses amounting to ten cents a day for each child. On this conservative assumption the 7,000 American religious serving abroad would need more than twenty-five million dollars a year to support their ministries.

Another indication may be gained from the audited report of the Religious Communities Trust, an organization referred to later in this article. In 1976–77 some sixty different congregations deposited thirty-five million dollars with the Religious Communities Trust. These short-term deposits represent, for the most part, monies to be spent for the apostolic activities of these communities. If we project that amount to the approximately 500 major provinces in the United States we obtain a figure of about three hundred million dollars of cash available for short-term investments.

LAND ASSETS

Centuries of experience have shown religious that they cannot carry on their apostolates and sustain themselves relying on the donations and stipends of each month. Efforts were made to establish permanent sources of income to fund these needs. For the most part these early investments involved ownership of real estate. The produce of the land was sold, the land itself was rented or buildings were leased.

In addition to real estate held for investments, religious congregations purchased or were bequeathed large tracts of land on which they built their general and provincial administration offices, novitiates, scholasticates and infirmaries. These holdings, once inexpensive rural property, today may be very valuable. Many of the buildings are almost deserted due to reduced numbers of candidates, or moving to more adequate facilities. The lands and buildings are listed on a balance sheet as an asset but they may be a heavy cash liability. Increasingly governments are taxing real estate holdings by religious, especially when unused. Care and protection of these facilities is expensive. Their size and age frequently mean that they have no market value. From the viewpoint of responsible stewardship, the retention of unproductive or costly real estate is wasteful. Catholic religious congregations are land-rich and cash-poor. It is not unusual to find charitable institutions with real estate assets worth many millions of dollars facing severe financial crises, including bankruptcy, because of inability to meet payments on a relatively small debt. Real estate assets are not easily marketable. Lending institutions are reluctant to accept religious oriented property as collateral. A growing number of congregations find their real estate an albatross around their neck. Their financial condition is difficult, even dangerous, because they are short on liquid assets. In a 1973 survey of Catholic institutions in the United States, more than two-thirds of the respondents admitted they were in the process of selling real estate. Unfortunately, much of this activity was to meet current claims rather than prudent provision against future liabilities.

INVESTMENTS

Most religious congregations today have funded some of their current and future liabilities by investments in securities. Generally these investments are designated for specific obligations, such as debt reduction, or education of candidates. Funds received for mission activities are spent for current operations. Congregations with institutions serving the public, such as schools and hospitals, often have endowment funds for these institutions. Since these service institutions generally give a public accounting of their finances, the size of such endowment funds is known. The investments which help support the religious themselves and which sustain some of their ministries are generally not known. The size of these investments varies considerably from one province to another. The author's personal estimate is that in the United States there is close to two billion dollars in investments for religious congregations or roughly ten thousand dollars for each religious. Considering the community needs and apostolic services to be funded, this is a small sum. Investment returns average perhaps 8% of the annual income of a community.

SALARIES AND STIPENDS

Remuneration for services rendered account for roughly 60% of a congregation's income. The daily mass stipend is a substantial part of the income for congregations or priests. Many priests in monastic orders, missionary congregations and communities of itinerant preachers have no other regular income. Not infrequently one finds a missionary priest who supports himself entirely with the money he receives from mass stipends, plus seasonal gifts of food from his parishioners.

In a few countries religious engaged in health and educational apostolates receive an equitable salary from the State. But for other ministries the monetary returns hardly support the apostolic worker. Some diocesan regulations stipulate that religious workers, especially sisters, receive a smaller remuneration than the diocesan clergy. Congregations whose members perform non-salaried services (inter-parochial or inter-diocesan apostolates, mission activities, preaching, and so on), and depend on free-will offerings of the faithful, fare even worse. Religious congregations must rely on other sources to supplement their income in order to meet both internal community and external apostolic needs.

DONATIONS

The contributions of benefactors are an important source of income for religious congregations. Donations and bequests practically support the apostolic services of religious in developing countries and are an essential supplement to sustaining these ministries in more affluent societies. Contributions, especially larger ones, are often for a designated project. Sometimes money is given in response to an appeal for a specific need. But many benefactors, especially close friends of the congregation, make their donations without restriction, permitting superiors to use these monies for administrative purposes, care of the community or support of the apostolate. Donations frequently constitute as much as 30%–45% of the annual budget of a religious congregation.

A number of religious congregations have carefully organized appeal programmes. Many orders, especially clerical groups, have formed associations whose members share in certain spiritual benefits or have specified prayers said for them each day or week or month. The stipend for enrollment in these associations is a way of contributing to the support of the religious congregation and its apostolate.

MANAGEMENT

Until recently management of finances in a religious congregation was very informal and comparatively simple. The author recalls two decades ago when the general treasurer of a large congregation showed him the monthly account, income and expenses, written on the inside of used envelopes. Today, however, treasurers on provincial and generalate levels are rapidly becoming aware of the need for professionalism in the management of the assets entrusted to their congregations. Very few treasurers in religious congregations have a degree in business administration, although, in the United States a growing number of sisters have professional qualifications. Women treasurers in the United States have formed a national Conference of Religious Treasurers (CORT) with fifteen active regional groups. Treasurers in male congregations have organizations in Washington and Chicago. Italy has a somewhat similar organization called the Centro Nationale Economi di Comunitá.

For the most part, however, there is great reluctance to accept professional standards of performance and control. Administrative boards (general and provincial councils) do not see the need for these standards. Changes in business management procedures are, in general, accepted only under pressure from lending institutions, government regulations or economic crisis. The latter motive is often a case of closing the barn door after all the horses have escaped. Too readily the evaluation of a friend or, even worse, of an interested party is taken as assurance that all is well in the area of business management.

Recognition of the need for quality assistance has prompted the creation in the United States of Stewardship Services Incorporated and Religious Communities Trust. Both organizations were founded by religious and are controlled by boards of trustees composed of religious from various orders. The administration of the organizations, however, is in the hands of professionals. Stewardship Services Inc. is an advisory and information service. It organizes workshops, publishes bulletins and financial journals for its members, suggests standards of performance and control, acts as a catalyist for co-operative programmes and places religious treasurers in contact with professional services. About one hundred religious congregations are members.

Religious Communities Trust is a money-market trust organized exclusively to assist treasurers in the management of their surplus funds. Funds deposited with RCT are invested only in short-term fixed-income securities of the highest quality. During 1977 participants in Religious Communities Trust earned 5.98% on their funds. In addition to this attractive yield treasurers can deposit or withdraw funds at any time.

BUDGETS

Budgeting is an essential instrument for planning and management. Yet many congregations and provinces do not use budgets. A surprising number of religious are unacquainted with budgets, view them as unnecessary and as an unwarranted restriction.

Often enough where there is a budget it is not used as an instrument for planning and management. In a growing number of communities, however, budgeting is used to identify foreseeable needs and income, establish priorities and allocate funds. Participation in the process of preparing a budget and of periodic reviews is a most effective exercise of co-responsibility. Interestingly enough, many groups have found the budget process an important building block for strengthening community life.

ACCOUNTING

The simple accounting procedures in religious congregations were adequate for a situation where income exceeded expenses. With the need to borrow money, to service debts, to manage for future liabilities, administrators today require accurate and meaningful financial statements. In some parts of the world accounting practices in religious congregations follow professional standards. But in many places the accounting is in initial stages of development.

Some large congregations employ lay-people as accountants. Although only a few religious are certified public accountants, many others, especially sisters in the United States and Canada, have studied accounting. Generally, however, the religious appointed to act as accountant has little or no preparation. At best there is on the job training in following the system which has been used for years with apparent satisfaction.

Only a minority of religious congregations in North America have an independent audit of their internal financial records. In other parts of the world such an audit appears to be almost unknown. With growing frequency, chapters and lending institutions are requiring an annual audit. It is a rare community accountant or business manager who has not found an audit beneficial. In a number of instances auditors have been able to help communities avert serious problems.

REPORTING

Each province within a religious congregation has a system whereby the individual houses report their financial condition to the central province administration. Such reports are usually issued monthly or quarterly. At times reports are either too detailed or so general as to be useless. Often the reports are filed away in the provincial office without being studied. In some provinces, however, the accountant or treasurer studies these statements and makes a presentation to the council regarding them. Good reports list both the budgeted and the realized figures.

Within international communities the reports from the provinces to the generalate are often of dubious value. These reports are made annually or, sometimes, every three or four years on the occasion of a provincial chapter. Some provinces prepare clear and helpful reports; others are confused and ambiguous. It is difficult to prepare a financial questionnaire or report-form which corresponds to the economic system in different countries or which will be understood uniformly in several cultures and languages. Clerical communities tried printing their financial forms in Latin. This was uncertain at best and proved increasingly unsatisfactory.

Some provinces prepare a consolidated balance sheet, showing all the financial operations belonging to the province. Few generalates prepare such a consolidated report of the assets and liabilities of the entire institute. In connection with this observation it is interesting to note that the information requested by the Holy See in the present annual report does not include a financial statement. Not even the Holy See is privy to information on the financial condition of religious congregations.

CONTROLS

Canonical legislation on the permissions required for various types of transactions is in dissaray. A number of church authorities and canonical experts in Anglo-Saxon countries, for example, simply say that much of the legislation is not applicable to their economic situation or to existing civil laws. This opinion seems particularly common in the United States and Canada. The hierarchy of the United States, for example, has not established any figure for the amount of borrowing or selling beyond which permission must be obtained from the Holy See. The canonical concept of conveyance (also called alienation) appears incompatible with modern fiscal realities. At best there is massive confusion over the interpretation and application of canonical legislation in regard to selling and borrowing. Religious, especially religious women, complain that there are two standards or interpretations of law: one for congregations of religious women and another for bishops and religious men.

The controls internal to a religious congregation vary, depending upon the degree of centralization. Two basic systems are in common use. One method employs budgets. The local community prepares an annual budget and then sends it to the provincial authority where it is reviewed and, if necessary, modified to co-ordinate with the overall province budget. Province budgets will be submitted to general authority for approval. Province budgets are rarely modified to bring them into coordination with any congregation-wide budget. Once approved, by provincial or general authority, expenditures contained in the budget are authorized. Each congregation has norms regulating the acceptance of designated donations, limiting transfer of expenditures within an approved budget and, especially, restricting disbursements beyond those approved.

Another popular system is to define expenditures as being either ordinary or extraordinary. Each congregation declares certain types of financial transactions forbidden, at least if they exceed a specified amount. Examples of these restricted transactions, often called 'extraordinary expenses,' might be borrowing money, selling land, purchasing an automobile or altering the structure of the religious house. Up to a certain amount permissions for such transactions may be granted on the provincial level. Beyond that sum the 'extraordinary expense' must be approved by the general government. This system works well in controlling large or unusual expenditures but is a weak instrument for management. In other areas local groups may spend freely whatever money is available to them. Provincial administrators must seek to persuade local communities to limit their expenditures for the sake of some other provincial programme or priority. Effective planning is weakened.

INTERNAL SHARING

Few organizations, including other Christian Churches, are as highly decentralized in their control of finances as the Catholic Church. Yet not only Catholic laity but also many religious and priests assume that there is national or international control of church finances at some high level. The truth is that when it comes to the ability to effect the transfer of a dollar bill from one diocese to another or from one religious congregation to another, Catholic entities are as independent as sovereign states.

Even within the same religious congregation the sharing of material goods from one house to another or, especially, from one province to another, is quite limited. In some congregations, especially among sisters, there is rather generous sharing of resources between the religious houses of the same province. In these institutes the provincial authority freely collects all the excess funds held by the various affiliated houses. Provinces with this type of sharing are introducing centralized banking, with all accounts of affiliated houses deposited in one central bank fund. The pooled money is then invested until checks arrive at the central bank for disbursement of funds. In many congregations, however, the fiscal autonomy of local groups within a province is very strong. Apart from a carefully regulated tax to support the programmes and services of central authority (provincial or general) the monies received or earned by the religious of a particular local community belong to and remain in the ownership of that local house.

Apart from a limited right of taxation, few generalates of international congregations have effective authority to move monies from one province to help another province. Often enough the constitutions of the congregation explicity affirm this authority for the superior general, but the reality of the situation makes its exercise impossible. Government regulations, desires of donors, province projects and human emotions combine to prevent any such movement of monies. In at least a few instances where this authority has been invoked the despoiled province has felt injured and appealed to the Holy See. The resulting hurts and disagreements tend to make such provisions of constitutions more a devout ideal than an administrative norm.

PROVINCE ASSESSMENTS

Each province within a congregation will have a number of programmes and services which benefit the entire province. Even though some of these services may be performed in one particular religious house they are for the benefit of the entire province. Formation of new candidates and care of the sick or elderly are common examples. Other services, particularly communication and presence, are necessary for the unity, development and effectiveness of the province as an apostolic community. As a necessary result of decentralization there is a call today for more of such services and supports on the part of provincial authority.

Funding these province programmes and services, including provincial government itself, requires substantial amounts of money. Provincial offices seldom receive the stipends or salaries of the religious, as they go directly to the local community to which the religious belongs. An exception to that would be religious on special apostolic assignment and living apart from other members of the congregation (e.g., chaplains, teachers in state schools). Usually these religious send their salary directly to the provincial authority. The bulk of the money needed to underwrite these various programmes and services has to come from several sources. One source is donations or bequests made directly to the province entity rather than to an affiliated house. Investment income is another means of meeting these expenses. Generally, however, a programme of taxation is necessary to obtain income for these province activities. Occasionally the provincial administration levies a specific tax for each of the services (e.g., education, retirement, insurances, administration, province meetings, and so on) for which the central administration pays. In this way the religious understands what the tax is used for and sees the amount collected for a specific service. The local community is taxed either on the basis of each resident in the house or for each active member of the community. Even within this system it may be necessary to have an assessment for some items, such as deferred maintenance on a building fund, based upon ability of the particular house to pay. Other provinces simply determine an annual sum which each active religious must send to the provincial administration. In provinces where the sharing is strong, the provincial authority either establishes one lump assessment for each house based upon ability to pay, or takes all monies left over after the monthly bills have been paid.

The amount needed by a provincial administration will vary considerably, depending upon the services performed and the other sources of income. As a conservative estimate, provinces in Western Europe and North America will probably have to receive somewhere between $1,500 and $2,000 a year from each religious to maintain the necessary programmes and services.

SUPPORTING GENERAL ADMINISTRATION

As a rule, generalates of international congregations provide few programmes for services of direct benefit to the individual religious.

Some generalates are responsible for a centralized educational programme but ordinarily expenses are limited to supporting the general council and staff. Travel and publications may be the only large expenses other than the normal cost of living. Due to the physical remoteness of general administration and the indirect nature of the services rendered, it is often difficult for generalates to obtain the necessary funds.

All international generalates depend upon monies received from the provinces. Contributions from benefactors to the general administration are almost non-existent. Few generalates have investment income. Three different methods appear to be used to obtain these funds.

One method is to assign an assessment for each religious in the province. Obviously such an assessment will vary from province to province according to a prudent estimate of the financial capability of the province. For provinces in the third world this might be as low as one dollar a month for each religious. Provinces in the major economic countries of Europe and North America might be assessed at ten to fifteen dollars a month for each religious.

A second manner of taxation is somewhat similar. The general administration establishes a quota for each province, prescinding from any explicit reference to the number of religious. This determination is based upon the gross annual income of a province and the quality of its expenses. Provinces which are able to underwrite development projects or fund future liabilities, for example, would receive a larger quota than a province whose income was consumed in providing necessities for the religious.

A third system, in some clerical congregations, permits use of the same norms found in either of the other two but does not necessitate the payment of cash to the generalate. The generalate sends a number of mass intentions to each province but retains the stipend for these intentions. Typically, for instance, a moderately solvent province in Southern Europe might receive three or four mass intentions a month for each religious. The province is responsible for celebrating masses for these intentions and the generalate retains the offering which accompanied the request. Basic to this system is the assumption that several provinces receive more requests for masses than they are able to satisfy and they second these extra intentions to their generalate.

A word should be added about support for the mission activities of religious congregations in developing churches. The more common organizational structure is that a particular province assumes responsibility for providing personnel and finances for a specific mission area. In some congregations, particularly missionary institutes founded in the last century, responsibility for these missions rests directly with the general administration. Naturally, therefore, control of the money received to support these missions resides with the superior general.

CONCLUSION

It would be misleading to conclude this article without at least mentioning the serious economic plight facing many congregations. A rising average age in their membership makes heavy demands on the income of a reduced number of apostolic workers. In many countries government regulations have cut into income. Salaries and, especially, free will offerings for the services of religious do not increase with the cost of living. Inflation is strong almost everywhere, rampant in some countries. All of these factors create problems for religious congregations. As difficult as these circumstances are, however, I am convinced that the two factors which will prove most damaging to the economic health of religious congregations are their tenacity in retaining unnecessary and unproductive lands or buildings and their complacency in continuing administrative procedures incompatible with responsible stewardship.

PART II

Problems Arising in the Financial Structures

Vincent Cosmao

The Church and Aid
to Developing Countries

> And I tell you, make friends for yourselves by means of unrighteous
> mammon, so that when it fails they may receive you into the eternal
> habitations.   Luke 16:9

WHEN, in the early 1960s, the FAO (the United Nations Food and
Agriculture Organization) launched its 'world campaign against
hunger,' which was to become in the 1970s, 'action for development,'
the churches in the industrialized countries set up new organizations to
coordinate Catholic participation in the campaign. There was thus established a new network for the transfer of funds from the industrialized to the developing countries: CIDSE, International Co-
operation for Socio-Economic Development, an international working
party within which Catholic organizations for aiding development tried
to plan and put into operation a common strategy for their Churches'
commitment to the battle for development.

Unlike the Propagation of the Faith, the work of St Peter the Apostle, the Society of the Holy Childhood, and other bodies that originated
in initiatives from below but were then taken over by the Holy See;
unlike Caritas Internationalis which originated from the federation of
national works of charity, and became with a flourish of Paul VI's pen
in Populorum Progressio (46) 'our' Caritas Internationalis, though it did
not become a part of the Holy See; unlike the pontifical Council Cor

Unum, a body of the Holy See's set up in 1971 to coordinate the whole of 'charitable aid, assistance, and development' in order to 'promote human and Christian progress,' while still 'preserving the special character and executive responsibilities of each organization'; [1] unlike all these, CIDSE is, at least at present, a 'regional' organization of the Catholic Church for which the episcopates of the various countries represented on it are responsible.

There is always a certain dialectical tension with the logic of centralization, even when that centralization is directed to ensuring 'a fraternal and continuous exchange, not only among those who have the goods and money to give, but also between them and those who, having a right to receive a share, also have the right to a say in how it should be used.'[2] The CIDSE, by the very way it is constituted, has had the necessary flexibility to adapt rapidly and empirically to the requirements of the work for development—work of which it became clear over the years that aid, in the sense of handing over cash, could not be the principal moving force, even though it might often remain the necessary condition. Consequently, the member organizations of CIDSE, or at least several of them, have developed over the past ten years in a way that can best be described as turning from charitable action to political action, with the education of public opinion in the industrialized countries becoming their number one objective.[3] Aid has hence become integrated into a global strategy which may be capable of neutralizing the effects of dependence that almost inevitably result from it.

That change is in line with the way world thinking about development has evolved, and it is the corollary of the fundamental change that has gradually made two things clear: first, development cannot be planned and put into effect except by societies that re-construct themselves by regaining control of their own dynamic; and second, it demands a transformation of the relationship between countries that have achieved industrialization and those that are excluded from it.

To understand this change we must examine in turn: 1. what constitutes under-development; 2. the notion of development as a process of the reconstruction of societies from within; 3. the transformation of international structures upon which that development depends, or from which it will result. Only then will it be possible to evaluate: 4. the connexion to be observed in the Church's activity between giving financial aid and arousing public opinion.

Under-development is a process whereby societies are de-structured by being polarized by industrial society

As long as under-development was seen as a state of economic, social and cultural backwardness resulting from technological backwardness, then development aid, in the form of injections of technology, know-how and capital was obviously the natural way to deal with it—whether the motives of the groups committed to such aid were those of humanitarian or charitable solidarity, or merely directed to enlarging the market to permit economic growth.

Experience showed that, though such aid sometimes produced the possibility of economic take-off and increased modernity, it also accentuated the internal contradictions of the societies it disturbed, drawing them into a dynamic extraversion and thus of growing dependence. By entering the world market, they came to be more and more controlled by the decision centres of the world system.

This observation made it clear that it is the disturbance of societies by outside intervention that explains under-development, even though technological backwardness may be one element of the problem.

Whether one stresses the pillage[4] of natural and human resources, the enforced transformation of the modes and relationships of production, or the dependence resulting from accumulation on a world-wide scale,[5] the dynamic of under-development emerges, in the final analysis, as a process of de-structuring societies, in other words, of disintegrating the relationships that constitute them as societies. Such societies, having been for centuries structured by means of the relationships established among their various component groups, are now polarized by the dominant society, and see their internal relationships of exchanging goods—material or token—replaced by a series of unrelated links between their individual sub-sections and the centres of activity or power of the world system. All the structures—economic, social, political, cultural—that held them together as systems of relationships among groups collapse one after another, though the order may vary, until finally, sometimes visibly, we witness at the end of the process a veritable pulverization whereby people are transformed into derelicts. The chaotic fringes of the monster cities of the third world are a perfect illustration of this social disintegration. In some cases quite a short time has seen the various stages of de-structuring as the traditional village, transplanted to the edges of a town, became the shanty-town, utterly uprooted and with no prospect of being integrated into the fabric of the city. De-culturation, without any acculturation, is another measurable manifestation of how people are turned into a sub-proletariat in the final stages of under-development.

Technological backwardness is itself largely a consequence of this disruption of the social dynamic, for, at an earlier point in their history, these societies were capable of perfecting whatever techniques they needed to control their natural environment and organize themselves into societies. Indeed, no society can survive or reproduce itself without being able to produce the economic, social and cultural conditions necessary to its existence.

Development is a positive, willed action to re-structure societies

If under-development is this sort of process of disintegration, it is bound to worsen and gather momentum by the force of its own inertia. There can only be development, then, if the process is reversed, and a new process of re-structuring set going; both operations must be purposely undertaken from within, even though they may, in some circumstances, be inspired from outside.

A collective about-face of this kind can occur either at the level of small groups, or at that of nations in the making.

Starting from political independence and the State powers it brings into being, internal points of re-structuring can be established in a nation or a group of nations. It is vital that colonial status should not be succeeded by a neo-colonial one, and that State power should not be in the hands of groups that stand to gain from the preservation of dependence because they are part of the network and function as extensions or antennae of the dominant society. Recent history has shown that this is no imaginary risk: many of the countries we think of as having 'taken off' and being well on the way to development are merely on the way to being integrated into the fringes of the world system, to the benefit of their ruling classes and the detriment of their people.

But there are exceptions: there are countries engaged in varying degrees in development policies conducted by governments whose object is the re-structuring of the societies for which they are responsible. In the context of a collective project, they enforce the exertions and restraints of rationalization or planning that must be effected if everything possible is to be tried in terms of needs and potential.

This sort of re-structuring, originating with the State power that can impose the necessary constraints, is the more likely to be successful if the people actively support the government. For this to happen, there must also be changes in the smaller social groups whereby they regain control of their own affairs.

Experience has shown that it is generally at this level that the about-face process on which development depends is determined. Unlike forms of popularization that aim only at transmitting techniques or inculcating social skills, moves towards consciousness-raising that aim to help groups advance from a naive or resigned state of mind to one that is critical and creative [6] can stimulate the surge of energy they need to take charge of their own lives and return to managing their own relationships with their natural and social environment. What is needed, in fact, is a real reactivation or cultural revolution—something for which it is hard to achieve all the conditions.

When that comes, the tension between the State power and the mobilized and organized population could produce a dynamic for the reconstruction of society all over the world.

In a neo-colonial situation, on the other hand, antagonistic tensions can only become exacerbated. The circulation of information, the activity of agents not under State supervision, the advances in awareness among ordinary people, all contribute—at least where the process of under-development is not too far advanced—to mobilizing basic groups that are in a position to gain some control over the organization of their own production and exchange relations. This dynamic is bound to find itself in opposition to those forces that are integrated into the dominant system and have an interest in maintaining dependence. Such situations of tension are on the increase all over the world precisely to the extent that policies geared solely to economic growth in line with the world-wide system become more generally accepted.

Development necessarily involves a transformation of the world-wide system

If it is the organization of the whole world around the industrializing centre that has brought about the de-structuring of the societies on the periphery, then obviously any re-structuring will demand a reorganization (whether freely-chosen or enforced) of the existing relations among countries at differing stages of industrialization.

The international division of labour on the basis of 'comparative advantages' has not led to the generalized development for which its nineteenth-century proponents hoped: on the contrary, the development or enrichment of some has produced the under-development or impoverishment of others. It is no longer possible today to expect any expansion of development for the increasing number of countries that fall behind the growth of the centre. Furthermore, the transfer of resources to which the industrialized countries are committed (1% of the

GNP, of which 0.7% comes from government grants) has not been achieved as long as deliberate increases in the price of oil and other raw materials have not been followed by any massive flow of funds.

By determining to combine together in their aim to reappropriate their own natural resources and the control of the economic activities flowing from those resources (Algiers 1973), by 'arbitrarily' putting up the price of oil, the third world countries (non-aligned, and grouped since 1977 with the OPEC) have totally changed the terms of the problem by proposing world co-operation to establish a new international economic order (of the sixth extraordinary general assembly of the UN, 1974).

Since then, international life has been suspended before this threshold which the industrialized countries have lacked the political will to cross. Despite a proliferation of conferences, no effective negotiation has been achieved, and the contradictions that must be resolved have intensified: the relative costs of primary products and of manufactured products and services, the indebtedness of the developing countries, etc. The crisis in the industrialized countries, which the increase in the price of oil and other raw materials has illuminated rather than caused, is not just an accident, a hitch in the history of the industrial system. It is a sign that the effects of de-structuring produced at the periphery by the industrialization at the centre are now rebounding onto the centre itself. The low price of raw materials and of primary products in general, which is what made the kind of industrialization we have had possible, could not be maintained indefinitely once the contradictions inside the centre—capitalism/socialism/democracy— made overt despotic domination of the periphery no longer thinkable. When the countries that control energy, raw materials and certain primary products became powerful enough to impose their own conditions of supply and payment, the system entered a state of crisis: the relation between the value of primary products and the value added by processing and distributing them was bound to change unless the industrialized countries once again combined to impose *their* conditions for acquiring them, or developed substitute products that would make them once again independent of their suppliers. It is most unlikely, given the dead weight of habits formed in the days when they could exploit the producers from their position of power, that the industrialized countries will implement such policies soon enough to escape having to negotiate with their developing neighbours. (Unless the latter, fed up with the inability of the industrialized countries to negotiate, embark on a strategy of collective autonomy.)

As things stand (in early 1978), despite the stagnation of negotiations, a possible way out of the present impasse of the international system has been indicated by the proposal of the third world countries of a world-wide negotiation to establish a new international economic order.

In the long term, industrialized and developing countries both stand to gain by agreeing on conditions acceptable to them all. Indeed it is the industrialized that have the most to gain. But in the short term, what is most obvious is the conflict of interests: to pay the developing countries a juster reward for their labour will inevitably affect living standards and employment levels in the industrialized countries. Having lived beyond their means when they were all-powerful, they are going to be forced into a certain degree of moderation, if only as regards raising their standard of living.

It is becoming clearer and clearer that the industrialized countries— or at least those of them that cannot be self-sufficient—have everything to gain by entering the negotiating process proposed by the third world.

Financial aid and the need to arouse public opinion

In essence, relations between industrialized and developing countries can only be improved if public opinion in the industrialized countries can be brought to see beyond the short-term conflict of interests between the two to the long-term harmony of their interests, providing that an honest negotiation leads to the possibility of agreement over necessary compromises.

This change can only come about by dint of working to present and analyze the facts so that the public will be educated to envisage what would once have been unthinkable. Work of this sort presupposes a strategy that breaks away from immediate problems, whereas the authorities and all political and trade-union bodies are, because of the existing crisis, continually having to face immediate problems that must be resolved if they are not to become the prisoners of policies without any future.

In these circumstances, the churches are becoming the focus of a new social demand, somewhat unexpected in view of their marginal position in societies that came into being by shaking off their guardianship. Since there are no other agencies organized or mobilized to educate public opinion towards wanting to transform the relationship between industrialized and underdeveloped countries, the churches could do a great deal to foster the development of that political will upon which the reorganization of the world depends.

The role played by the churches, at least at first, in legitimating the reorganization of the world by, and for the benefit of, Europe, makes it a positive duty for them to contribute to making clear the total absence of legitimacy in the system that has been produced thereby—a system which, whatever progress it may have achieved in some places, has doomed the majority of the human race to under-development.

If the churches are to play this ideological rôle, it is vital 'that Christians be committed to living out their apostolic activity within their social and political activity, thus getting at the roots of the evil, transforming people's hearts at the same time as they transform the structures of modern society.' [7]

These are the lines along which the work of the CIDSE organizations are developing, associating the arousal of public opinion more and more closely with the giving of financial aid, and asking their opposite numbers in the third world whose work they are assisting with their money to help them in return by taking part in the work of information and education that they are involved in at home. Such reciprocal aid also contributes to the possibility of a 'co-management' between 'donors' and 'beneficiaries.' [8]

This process, even though at the moment it still exists only in embryo, is already significant enough to be seen as the first step towards a relationship totally different in kind from those that have been in operation since the fifteenth century.

For the future, the majority of Christians will be living in the third world. As changes in demographic balance coincide with the emancipation of the churches in 'mission lands,' the churches have come to constitute an international area in which the self-determination of nations, which is the necessary condition for development, may have some chance of being taken seriously. It will be so to the extent that the old churches, the churches of the centre, can recognize that the seat of power, including theological power, is shifting, in the Church as in the world.

In the dynamic of these changes, as can already be seen, the circulation of money will no longer *necessarily* produce the effects of domination that have been inevitable in a system in which money and power have been inseparable and far too unevenly distributed.

Translated by Rosemary Sheed

Notes

1. Letter, 'Amoris officio,' dated 15 July 1971 in *La Documentation Catholique*, no. 1592 (5 September 1971).

2. Paul VI, Allocution to the Pontifical Council 'Cor Unum' on 13 January 1972 in *La Documentation Catholique*, no. 1662 (6 February 1972).

3. I need hardly say that this interpretation is mine, and does not commit the CIDSE or its constituent organizations.

4. P. Jalee, *Le pillage du Tiers-monde* (Paris, 1971).

5. Cf., for instance, Samir Amin, *L'Accumulation à l'échelle mondiale* (Paris, 1970), 2 vols.

6. Cf., for instance, Paulo Freire, *The Pedagogy of the Oppressed* (New York & London, 1969).

7. Cf. n. 2, supra.

8. V. Cosmao, 'Transfert de fonds, de pouvoir et d'idées,' *Lumière et Vie*, 129/130 (1976).

Wim Rood

Co-operation and communion between the Churches. Some remarks from an interested observer

THE sequence in the heading, 'co-operation and communion,' is based on a practical consideration. For communion will only become clear as co-operation between the churches is being achieved.

One can start with communion in biblical and theological terms as a gift and mandate in Jesus Christ. The fundamental bond which unites the members of the mystical body of the Lord demands co-operation. This co-operation makes the communion, hidden at first, visible. My remarks apply to both these spheres of tension.

While the summary and evaluation of a study project of the Inter-University Institute for Missiology and Ecumenism in Leiden and Utrecht on mutual assistance between the churches in the perspective of the Missions by Dr. E. Jansen Schoonhoven (Leiden 1977) runs to 60,000 words I can offer the reader only a few remarks on points chosen from a vast theme.

THE EXTENSION OF CO-OPERATION AND COMMUNION FROM WITHIN THE CHURCH TO THE WHOLE WORLD

In the New Testament, particularly the Epistles of St Paul, one finds numerous expressions which relate to the co-operation of the communities in the preaching of the Gospel. Two clear illustrations of mutual assistance of churches in the period of the New Testament are the aid of the Antioch community given to that of Jerusalem (Acts 11:27–30) and the collection, organized by Paul in the communities he founded in Asia Minor and Greece for the poor of Jerusalem (Rom. 15:26–27; I Cor. 16: 1–3; II Cor. 8–9; Gal. 2:10; Acts 20: 4). The main pattern of these collections remains valid: material needs, making them known, active sympathy, contributions according to ability, mediating the transmission of the money entrusted to the church's leaders.

The ecumenical movement arose from the ecumenical missionary Conferences. It was precisely in the preaching of the Gospel and the *diakonia* towards non-Christians that the inter-Christian divisions were most acutely experienced. Co-operation in the field of serving society—the diaconate—is more easily achieved than combined evangelization because the latter, certainly in the case of Roman Catholic evangelization, aims at conversion, belief and the building up of the Church (Cf., *Ad Gentes* 12, esp. 15, but also 26 and 39).

The service of the world by the churches collectively—the world diaconate—is then extended to a service of the world together with all men and groups of good will who wish to change the 'face of the earth' in one way or another for the better. Such a co-operative relationship between believers and non-believers, ecclesiastical and non-ecclesiastical groups, aimed at a definite approach to welfare, can become so fascinating that it eclipses the church community in the mind of those believing participants who belong to a church. When then the wish arises to think together about motivation and inspiration, it does not easily lead to collective thinking and living according to the Gospel because this is not typical of all. People rather remain stuck at the level of humanism and socialism.

However, evangelically rooted witness in favour of the poor and their needs remains a spiritual ferment in all liberation theologies. The practice of the faith not only demands the disclosure of injustice, but the formation of the conscience, the change of mentality, and worship of the true God and Jesus Christ our Saviour. However radical one's political commitment may be it should not embrace and override every other human activity. For Christian politics cannot provide the ultimate meaning of life. When politics is taken, not as a means, but as an absolute, human freedom will be threatened by totalitarian tendencies (*Orientierung* 41, 1977, pp. 253–58).

The extension of mutual aid from originally local churches to churches of different denominations and from there to the whole of mankind grew out of the unification of the world, rapid communication, the publicity media, the ecumenical movement, the growing awareness

that the faith must not remain confined within the church but get practically involved in society, the appeal of Marxist ideology and the
criticism of the poor performance of 2000 years of Christianity.

SOLIDARITY

For a long time the churches developed an image, in both doctrine
and practice, of being immersed in the depths of the Trinity and not
doing justice to the realities of this earth. Theology and the Church
kept aloof from what was going on in the world and concentrated on
what was going on in heaven.

Since Christian civilization lost its external influence in Europe,
America and the third world, and the Gospel has been thrown on its
own power of persuasion there has appeared a rift between the Gospel
as a message concerned with an eschatological fulfilment and the future
of mankind on this earth and its survival in the next century. The
question of the relation of the Gospel to the world has become an
important issue for the future of the Church.

The Platonic neglect of the present world came to light when secular
topics began to penetrate theological thought and could no longer be
ignored. The 1960s saw the rise of theologies with a genitive: a theology
of the world, of secularization, of the death of God, of history, of
change, of revolution, of liberation, of politics and of the blacks . . .
These theologies brought home the fact that a number of questions the
theologian should deal with had disappeared from his syllabus. Outside
the Church these questions had been raised much earlier. Socialism
freed many parts of the world of large land-ownership and on this point
removed much unjust disparity between rich and poor. At the same
time another injustice sprang up in the socialist camp, a new form of
self-alienation, through which millions of people have been deprived of
their freedom of expression (J. Smolík, 'Die Theologie der Genitive' in
Communio Viatorum 3, 1976, pp. 139–40). Numerous action groups are
today appealing to all men of good will to stand by the deprived and
oppressed. In co-operation and communion between the churches this
idea of 'solidarity' expresses a commitment, an attitude, which, however, must be examined critically.

Solidarity is defined as the awareness of belonging together and the
readiness to face the consequences of this. The word is used by Marxists, Socialists and Christians. It has become an in-word. It is meant to
convey that one wants to identify with the poor, the persecuted, the
oppressed and the deprived. One accepts the consequences of this
solidarity by committing oneself in word and deed together with the
poor, the persecuted, the oppressed and the deprived in the struggle

against poverty and for freedom and justice. On the whole Christians see these aims in the same way as other men of good will and are prepared to form one front with Socialists and Marxists.

However, as soon as prisoners have been set free and the right to accommodation, protest, freedom of expression and just wages has been achieved, this solidarity ceases. The aim has been attained. But, Christians ought to have a higher aim, namely the freedom of the children of God, which Paul mentions: 'I think that what we suffer in this life can never be compared to the glory, as yet unrevealed, which is waiting for us. The whole creation is eagerly waiting for God to reveal his sons. It was not for any fault on the part of creation that it was made unable to attain its purpose, it was made so by God; but creation still retains the hope of being freed, like us, from its slavery to decadence, to enjoy the same freedom and glory as the children of God' (Rom. 8: 18–21).

Any believer who looks at solidarity as aiming at the freedom of the children of God, the life of the new man in Christ, will see that at this deeper level solidarity includes not only the materially poor, the deprived and the prisoners but the rich, the oppressors, and the persecutors who are all called to this same freedom of the children of God.

Marx has pointed out that the property-owning class also suffers from self-alienation: 'The property-owning class and the class of the proletariat show the same human self-alienation. But the former feels itself happy and secure in this self-alienation, experiences this alienation as their own power and finds there the appearance of a human existence; the latter feels itself crushed in this alienation and sees there its total lack of power and the reality of an unhuman existence' (*The Holy Family,* p. 1). Marx maintains that both classes must be freed from their self-alienation. So he suggests that the way is that of the class struggle. But he does not understand the deeper meaning of solidarity which points towards the freedom of the new man in Christ. It is precisely here that Christians should differ from others in their struggle for a better society. It is here that they should make their authentic contribution to the collective commitment to a better world. Although in the practical working out of this the achievement of concrete results precedes the achievement of spiritual values. A Christian should let this final perspective influence his commitment to solidarity.

ENCOURAGE ONE ANOTHER IN THE FAITH

While the good news may be the ultimate aim of mutual co-operation and communion, the actual work of the mission and evangelization has acquired many aspects. It is no longer a matter of just prayer, financial

and personal assistance. The matter of know-how has become impera-
tive, publicity and protest activities support the fight for justice, and
occasionally—sometimes still hesitantly—one begins to understand the
experience of a Christian life in somebody else. This last aspect of
mutual co-operation and communion needs closer consideration.

Publicity about people in the third world usually emphasizes the way
in which these people try to acquire or preserve their political independence, and how, economically speaking, they really develop or get
oppressed.

We hear much less about how they survive culturally or are uprooted
now that the tradition by which they lived has been put adrift through
contact with the West and the need for an accelerated modernization of
their society. We only know a little about their attitude to life, or how
they see suffering and death, time and the transitoriness of reality. We
are keen to interrogate the churches of the third world about their
social commitment and their political protest, or—in other terms—
about their lack of people and means. But we seem much less interested in the way they live their religion and how they feed and spell
out their Christian motivation. We ask what the churches of Chile,
Rhodesia and India do about the oppressed, the marginalized and the
poor. We practically never ask what it means to such a church to do all
this according to the example set by Jesus Christ, with reference to his
Father and God's plan for salvation; how they are aware of this Father
and how closely they keep to him and his plan for salvation (a reference
to an address given by Dr. J. van Nieuwenhove at the opening of the
missionary centre at Heerlen on 21.10.1977. Cf. *Missieaktie*, nr. 6,
1977, p. 5).

For the second world, which, though outside the old way of thinking
of mission and evangelization but obviously involved in the question of
mutual co-operation and communion between the churches, the same
holds.

Aid to churches in Socialist countries of Eastern Europe is still too
limited to prayer, material support and sometimes the sending of
theological literature. In recent years there has been constantly increasing information which testifies to the genuine Christian life lived
by Christians in Socialist countries. Their identification with the
crucified Christ, their experience of being outcasts of society, of having
lost historical privileges have taught them to concentrate on the
spiritual power of faith, prayer, love, loyalty and suffering. This has set
non-believers wondering, stimulates questioning and creates a sense of
trustworthiness. And so they have become the yeast in a way that had
not been foreseen.

Indications of this Christian life, which we can constantly read about or which we discover by visiting are not understood by the churches of the 'free West.' We apparently still lack the antennae we need to pick up these signals which we could use for our own salvation. Brothers and sisters of the first world still look on Christians in the third world as wards; Christians of the second world still seem to us too often to be poor persecuted creatures who deserve our pity . . .

FROM THE LOUD CALL FOR HELP TO THE PRESSING REQUEST NOT TO BE HELPED

The number of requests for material help which reach the well-to-do churches from all over the world are so vast that these wealthy churches cannot cope with them. Because the possibilities of providing real aid are limited, there has to be a choice and this means that one has to accept priorities. Anyone who has regularly to deal with this call for aid could draw up a map of world needs with fierce red spots for regions that clamour most loudly and, passing through places with a lighter hue, blanks for regions which don't reach us at all, either because there is no need or because people don't know either the way or the possibilities open to them to get in touch with aiding churches.

Collection schemes, based on the seasons when the appeal to people is most effective, tax reduction, pressure by the mass media, money-raising organizations, the automatic writing off of debts, central administration of monies that are coming in, commissions which in a businesslike way compare and select projects, computers which register requests, finances and projects—all these things turn this way of missionary aid into a well-oiled machine which diminishes the personal commitment of the faithful and threatens to make the sacrifice lose its inner value through a kind of painless childbirth as a non-personal event.

This undeniable efficiency is coupled with the disadvantage that centralization becomes economic rather than ecclesiological and this does not necessarily promote ideal relations between churches and nations (Vincent Cosmao, 'Transfert de fonds, de pouvoir et d'idées,' in *Esprit* 1976, pp. 119–26).

In recent years some churches in the third world have asked for a temporary or complete halt (moratorium) to financial and personal aid. Young churches want to build up their own identity and in this way reach communion with sister churches in the world. This idea of a moratorium is also inspired by the lack of vision and courage in the lasting dominating influence of the countries which undertake missionary work.

At the World Missionary Conference of Bangkok (1973) it was said that the moratorium idea has sprung 'from our failure to relate to one another in a way which does not dehumanize.' If in Bangkok the moratorium was still seen as a possibility in certain situations, the Assembly of the All Africa Conference of Churches in Lusaka (1974) called upon the African churches to get rid as soon as possible of their foreign funds and personnel as the only way of becoming truly African churches (Jansen Schoonhoven, *loc. cit.,* pp. 156–66). The episcopal synod of 1974, which was confronted with the moratorium idea, particularly by the Latin American countries, rejected it. But the bishops wanted the assistance of foreign missionaries to change. They stressed that the presence of these missionaries 'was the living sign of the universal church.'

Organizers of financial aid organizations in the donor countries feel that this call for independence is shocking. Without this unilateral financial aid they feel themselves suddenly left empty-handed and are faced with the question what they have to offer in terms of genuine Christian life now that the churches of Europe and North America are themselves passing through a grave internal crisis. Many faithful in the countries which traditionally dominated missionary activity are now looking for their own identity and ask themselves how they can be Christian in a welfare society. Basic communities wish to be free from centralizing rules and regulations. They want to shape their concrete situation themselves according to the Gospel. Without using the term, they, too, want a moratorium.

BY WAY OF CONCLUSION

On re-reading what has been said, I realize that these remarks on 'co-operation and communion between the churches' must be seen above all as a random choice and arrangement of copious data.

But with all the changes in the understanding of mission and evangelization there remains one constant factor: to bring and deepen the good news of Jesus Christ. It is a question of a persistent task for Christians, a task, which must be achieved with human means, even though we know that the true achievement of it will always remain unfulfilled.

Translated by Theo Westow

Louis Trouiller

The Church as Steward of the Poor

TO DESCRIBE the Church as the steward of the poor has an old-fashioned ring. But at least the phrase is an invitation to go back to one of the most venerable of all traditions, a tradition grafted upon the Gospel itself. In using it, we are also seeking to define the Church: for one of its major functions is to provide for the needs of the poor, to distribute among them the proceeds of what it administers in their name, to pass on to them what it gets for them from the rich. Tradition, as we shall see, meant precisely that: the Church could only possess things for the poor, in their name. And John XXIII used to recall that the Church was, and wanted to be, above all 'the Church of the Poor.'

But is it really? or is it more of a pious wish, a wish that is father to the thought? We must take a closer look. First, therefore, we must establish in broad outline what is actually happening. Then, after a brief survey of the Tradition, we shall be able to consider what stewardship for the poor might mean for the Church today. Even the word must be re-examined: the 'poor' in our world are both the pariahs of our industrialized societies, and those nations ground down by poverty and by the implacable logic of what we like to call development.

DOES THE CHURCH USE ITS RESOURCES TO HELP THE POOR?

In this *Concilium* there are articles considering this question from various different points of view (cf. especially the article by Vincent Cosmao on the Church and aid to developing countries). Initiatives are taken, and institutions carry out their work, both on a world-wide scale, and in local churches. It is not my object here to describe them

all or catalogue the good they do. Yet even so, doubts arise: is the
Church truly the steward of the poor? One does notice certain things,
about both the way that ministry is exercised and the goals it appears
more or less consciously to pursue, that leave one wondering.

On looking into the facts, on examining for instance particular dioceses or congregations, one finds that the proportion of gifts and investments earmarked for the poor represents only a small percentage
of the whole budget. It is not hard to see why: the Churches in western
societies are, relatively, a lot less well off than they were. For one
thing, their resources bear no relation to the rising cost of living, and do
not increase as rapidly as it does. At the same time, their burdens
increase more rapidly than those of other social groups. Over all, the
clerical and religious population is aging, and the cost of health and
social security continues to rise. Finally, there is less cash available,
and our responsibilities within the Church absorb the larger part of any
possible surplus: little is left to help the poor. When aid is given—
which it usually is, albeit sometimes on a modest scale—one then finds
oneself asking, What sort of aid? In most cases, it is for pastoral or
missionary purposes. We are readier to help the religious orders of
churches of the new Christian communities than to provide for the
needs of their people. In fact, it has been pointed out that this course of
action is in the nature of cultural and religious imperialism—that the
Church is investing money in consolidating and supporting a 'universal' theology and worship.

Obviously all this needs a lot of qualification, and the present *Concilium* provides us with some necessary information. However, sweep-
ing though these comments are, they are not without foundation, and
they lead us on to ask ourselves what ultimate aims are being pursued.
Stewardship is not neutral: the direction money flows in results from a
political decision. What determines that decision largely depends on
the means we have available, both financial and human means. Our
training as priests or religious, the ideology of our society, our place in
it, even our social origins predispose us to extend (if necessary with
certain adjustments) our own ecclesiastical, pastoral or religious organization rather than to favour the risk of sharing what we have with
the very poor. In addition to these factors, there are those implied by
the origin of our resources, which in the main associate us lith social
classes and mental outlooks more attached to conserving present
economic and political structures than to trying to make a juster world.
Whether we are aware of it or not, we still remain one of the pillars of
the established disorder, whatever signs of change may be visible in
certain areas, and even at a very high level. Such signs are still a

minority phenomenon, and at best can only as yet represent a promise for the future.

It must further be admitted that the Church seems to show a failure of adaptation in the method of its stewardship for the poor. Again, there are obviously variations. But, overall, the Church clings to a style of intervention that belonged to the Christian establishments of the past. These were, of course, set up to respond to the needs of a society in which helping the poor was the Church's responsibility. It has been hard for the Church to recognize that that responsibility now falls to public bodies. That large gaps still remain for the Church to fill there is no doubt, and its generosity in doing so is evident. Yet this cannot conceal the fact that the State now does what the Church used to do—which could be a great liberation. We must take stock of the socio-political changes around us. It is no longer acceptable to talk naively of all our 'good works' as 'charity' or 'stewardship for the poor.' Like everyone else, we have to use our judgment, and we must be prepared to analyze our world and our Church without complacency. A period of stringent evaluation—which has in fact been begun in a number of different places—is the first requirement for establishing a Church that is specifically a Church of the poor. Nor are we totally unequipped for that evaluation: Christian Tradition enables us to re-define our objective, while also showing us what is at stake and what the dangers of distortion. Armed with this knowledge, we should be better able to understand the present and plan for the future.

CHRISTIAN TRADITION

Jesus was close to God's poor, whose precarious situation and whose hope are expressed in the Magnificat. It is to them that he announced the Good News of the Kingdom. As a poor man himself, he invited all who would follow him to get rid of their possessions. Hence, the poor, more than any other human beings, are his representatives and should be his disciples. Furthermore, the Christian must imitate him, must be animated by the same feelings; it is love that authenticates the disciple's life, above all, his relationship of love with the poor. The communities of the early Church lived that love intensely. Among other things, they understood the close bond Jesus established between service of the brethren and the eucharistic meal. In setting up the New Covenant, Jesus wants his disciples to build up the Kingdom by sharing everything together. Thus, the eucharistic meal becomes the sacrament of the Church, the fraternal community, which is itself—by its love put into practice, by its help to the poor—a sign in the world that the Kingdom is coming. This is the very core of the Christian life:—to love as Jesus loved, and those whom he loved, is what makes the Christian disciple and the Christian community.

As we know, sharing our possessions and helping the poor soon required an organization. The clergy rapidly found themselves handling ever larger amounts of goods given to the Church for the poor. It was always to be made clear that the Church possessed things only for them, administering in their name and for their benefit the goods it received. This principle was insistently recalled, and the Church endeavoured to observe it; throughout its history, saints and institutions adapted Christ's teaching to suit changing circumstances, and repeated the primitive commitment in their own ways. However, though the principle was reiterated, it must be admitted that there was a gradual deterioration. As early as the fifth century, Pope Gelasius divided the Church's goods into four: for the bishop (who was to succour pilgrims and captives), for the rest of the clergy, for worship, and for the poor. This division was carried on over the centuries, but the reality was not so good: what has been described as a veritable 'misappropriation of offerings' [1] began with Judas, soon followed by Ananias and Saphira . . . The causes of the decline are various, but it would seem that the major one was the institutionalization of the service of the poor. It certainly had to *be* organized, and the organization had its effectiveness. But at a heavy cost: the Church became a power, and even at one period, *the* power in Europe. In a sense, it is only now beginning to recover. The preaching of the Gospel did indeed inspire Christians to generosity, but the institution continued to grow heavier and make greater demands (the cost of services, of buildings, of administration), while the appetites of many high-ranking clerics, princes and other powerful people grew in proportion. 'The purity of the desire of the faithful' thus compromised the 'purity of the institution.' [2] The poor came to get no more than the crumbs—1% of the Church's income here, 3% there. Such figures 'caused more scandal than the charity itself caused edification.' [3] It is interesting to note that, in urging an end to these abuses, contemporaries referred back to the original principle: the Church's patrimony belongs to the poor; having embezzled the wealth it owed to the poor, it is still reaping the fruits of its misconduct.

There is another feature that marks this long history. With very few exceptions, neither Christians nor clergy have ever sought to understand *why* people are poor. Discussions about poverty, even among the critically-minded, have only referred to the organization of the Church. The social phenomenon, as such, was never recognized: poverty was too prevalent, and worsened with increasing urbanization, especially from the Renaissance onwards. It would appear that the Church, wholly occupied with itself, did not seek to understand the lives of others. With the approach of the French classical period, this impression becomes even stronger. The gulf between the Church and society became so enormous that when, in the nineteenth century, clear-sighted Christians denounced what was then called pauperization, they were simply not heard at all—other voices were far too loud. But to those other voices the Church would not listen, considering them a threat to its influence and its power, and quite unaware that that influence and power were already beginning to decline.

I fully realize that these are hard words. But at least this reminder of the evils of the past will enable us both to understand the roots of the present discrepancies between the declared ideal of a Church for the poor and the existing reality, and at the same time to recover the perspective of the early Church, while avoiding the mistakes of the past. For the Church, and for each one of us, it is a question of getting back to the sources in order to make the Kingdom come through loving and serving the poor in the world of today.

PROSPECTS

We know now that the existence of the poor is not a law of nature. Our world has been increasing with ever more widespread poverty— remembering that by 'poor' we understand all those excluded from growth and development, whether they live in the developing or the industrial countries. The poor are everywhere, and we know it. This is a first important change: in the past, the poor for whom the Church was steward were either Christians, or lived in a Christian world. The universality of poverty, in all its various forms, presents the problem in a new way, in that help can no longer be the business of Christian agencies alone, nor can it any longer be limited to pragmatic and *ad hoc* solutions. It seems clear that development causes inequity and marginalization, both in our own and in the developing countries. There are plenty of analyses of this phenomenon, and it is vital that we Christians take part in research into the causes of the growing disparity among nations, classes and individuals. Orthodox Marxism seems specious in both theory and practice, yet liberal and related doctrines have proved illusory and ineffective. It is undoubtedly the nature of the development that needs questioning.

It would seem that the prevailing economism or—which amounts to the same thing—productivism is at the root of the spread of poverty. It is fashionable to execrate the consumer society; yet what is it but the result of our worship of productivity—of goods that can only be consumed, or even wasted, without doing anything to make human beings and societies any freer to live and create? Economic criteria alone are not enough. Economy can never be a sound basis for politics. It is this that is the evil of our industrial societies (in both East and West), the evil with which we are polluting the rest of the world as we destroy all other cultures. There is nothing original about saying this. Let me quote in support the strong words of the representative of the Holy See to the United Nations Conference on Trade and Development of 1972 in Santiago: Adjustments are not enough, he said: 'the structures themselves must be changed, for these structures reflect and preserve intolerable inequalities. Behind the structures there is also a power system that must be reformed and transformed in such a way as to achieve an equitable sharing of responsibilities.'

This demand is not specific to the Church. More and more voices are being raised at international conferences to call for a new international economic order. Indeed it seems clear that what is wanted is a new order pure and simple—in other words, a new political order: what Ivan Illich has called a 'convivial society.'

The relative poverty of our Churches, which I spoke of at the beginning, should seem in the circumstances to be something of a stroke of luck. With all mankind, and with no more ready-made solutions to hand than anyone else, we have to create a world of brotherhood. All we know, in faith, is that Jesus of Nazareth subverted the established disorder in his day, and that we must follow him in giving an account of our hope and our charity: to know God is to love. It is up to us to share with the rest of the poor in discovering the new world. Strong in the Gospel and the Spirit, the Church can do great things at its own level when it translates into modern terms the truth it knew intuitively when it was founded, as well as ideas that have come to mind since then. But it still needs to be put into action. It is abundantly clear that we shall only be listened to, and credible, and effective as stewards for the poor if we practice what we preach. We shall only be able to share in subverting the oppression of the modern world in so far as we become converted to the Gospel by subverting what is evil in our own behaviour.

We must complete our own liberation from the burdens of the false power that has hampered the mission of the Church. We must get rid of all traces of imperialism—whether in theology, pastoral theory, or worship. We no longer have to defend the sort of authority that set the Church on a par with other political powers. What we must do is to de-institutionalize love: a formidable problem but, as history has shown, a vital preliminary to any genuine stewardship for the poor. It will undoubtedly mean that such service will no longer be the prerogative of clergy and religious. Like the apostles, they are called to other tasks. We may hope that this will mean the disappearance of that greed of possessions and love of property that have been so largely at the root of the abuses mentioned earlier. The Christian people as a whole will then take an active part in working to study and to resolve the problem: no longer will laymen have contributions to make only if they are in positions of power.

Finally, in its new form, the stewardship for the poor will be also administered *with* the poor. If we want to share our hope, we must share the poverty and the hope of the poor. We must ourselves pass by way of poverty: this is not because poverty is a good in itself—for it is a scandal and a disaster—but because only from a position of poverty can we fight its causes and make our protest in the name of love and of hope. Clearly the task ahead will be a hard one for the Church; we know all too well, from the experience of many of our own brethren as well as many other people, how fearful it will be in our world of blood and money. Yet Christ, who draws all things to himself, has told us that to hope for a world-wide society of brothers is not vain. It is with his Spirit that we must continue the work of analysis and reflexion begun by such men as Johann Baptist Metz, Jürgen Moltmann, Gustavo Gutiérrez, Leonardo Boff, and so many others. With him we must continue the conversion and liberation of and with the poor that some of our brethren have undertaken, with others, in Latin America and eastern Europe, in our countries and our churches. This, it seems to me, must be the prime object of our energy today: to participate, in our churches and our society, in the emergence of a juster world.

Readers may be surprised that I have not stressed material aid. It exists, of course, and as I have said, it was from the first to be without limit or ambiguity. It is clear that it must continue, both because there is still urgent need for it, and as an expression of generosity. In any case, economic aid will always be the criterion of authenticity of a more reflective, more political activity—that of sharing the condition of the oppressed. But it must be insisted that a flow of money alone is not all that is needed—twenty centuries have taught us that. Furthermore, as I have said, it looks as though the Church is losing and will continue to lose its financial power. This is a fact. It is also a hope.

In losing that, the Church will be able to recover its force for prophecy, and to make an effective contribution to the coming of a more fraternal human society. In losing its financial power, it will be able truly to preach the Gospel to the poor. Rather than being their steward, it will become their servant, and their sister.

Translated by Rosemary Sheed

Notes

1. M. Brion, 'La Paroisse dans l'Organisation financière de l'Eglise,' *Lumière et Vie*, 123 (1975), pp. 37–51.

2. G. Le Bras, *Les Institutions Ecclésiastiques de la Chrétienté Médiévale*, Fliche et Martin, *Histoire de l'Eglise depuis les Origines jusqu'à nos jours*, vol. XII, Part I, Books II–IV, pp. 252ff. (Paris, 1959).

3. G. Le Bras, op. cit., p. 582.

Walter Bayerlein

The Role of the Laity

THE THEOLOGICAL PRINCIPLES

The Position of the laity in general

THE Second Vatican Council rediscovered the rôle of the laity in the Church. In many places the Council stresses the important and unique contribution of the laity to the renewal of the Church.

I shall quote only a few significant statements as an indication of the emphasis placed by the Council on the fraternal collaboration of the various ministries within the one people of God: 'And if by the will of Christ some are made teachers, dispensers of mysteries, and shepherds on behalf of others, yet all share a *true equality* with regard to the dignity and to the *activity* common to all the faithful *for the building up of the Body of Christ*' (*Lumen Gentium*, 32).[1] 'The laity are gathered together in the People of God and make up the Body of Christ under one Head. Whoever they are, they are *called upon*, as living members, to expend *all their energy* for the *growth* of the Church and its *continuous sanctification*. For this very energy is a gift of the Creator and a blessing of the Redeemer. The lay apostolate . . . is a participation in the saving mission of the Church itself. Through their baptism and confirmation, *all are commissioned* to that apostolate *by* the Lord Himself' (*Lumen Gentium*, 33).

'Let sacred pastors *recognize* and promote the dignity as well as the *responsibility of the layman* in the Church. Let them willingly *make use of his prudent advice*. Let them *confidently* assign duties to him in the service of the Church, allowing him *freedom and room for action.* Further, let them encourage the layman so that he may undertake tasks on his own initiative' (*Lumen Gentium,* 37).

The view the Council puts forward here is by no means new. It has a solid basis in the New Testament (cf. Mt 23:8; 1 Cor. 12) and is rooted in the history of the first Christian communities (cf. Acts 11:19ff; 18:26; Rom. 16:1–16; Phil. 4:3). This view of the position of the laity directly implies the demand that all the baptized and confirmed should share the responsibility for carrying out the mission of the Church in the modern world.

It is regrettable that this demand is frequently seen one-sidedly as an exaggerated call to the Church authorities for 'democratization.' In fact it is chiefly a call for commitment on the part of all Christians, and only secondly a call to the Church authorities to give scope for a practical and effective share in responsibility by the laity. A share in responsibility without a share in the processes of decision making in the Church inevitably leads to impotent suffering at failures in the Church on which one can exercise no inftuence.

The Joint Synod of Dioceses in West Germany has put this very clearly in its resolution on the 'Responsibility of the Whole People of God for the Mission of the Church,' which is very important for our purposes:[2] 'The Church's responsibility to be the agent of Christ's saving mission is shared by the whole community and each of its members. No one can exclude himself, or be excluded, from this common responsibility' (I, 1.4). 'This requires all to work together as partners. To make this possible, structures for sharing responsibility are needed in which the common responsibility of all can be put into practice in different ways, corresponding to their position and gifts' (I, 1.6).

The Council had the highest hopes of the contribution this new emphasis on partnership between ministers and laity could make to the renewal of the Church: 'A great many benefits are to be hoped for from this familiar dialogue between the laity and their pastors: in the laity, a strengthened sense of personal responsibility, a renewed enthusiasm, a more ready application of their talents to the projects of their pastors. The latter, for their part, aided by the experience of the laity, can more clearly and more suitably come to decisions regarding spiritual and temporal matters. In this way, the whole Church, strengthened by each one of its members, can more effectively fulfill its mission for the life of the world' (*Lumen Gentium,* 37 end).

There are naturally many passages in the Decree on the Laity which could develop this idea, but we have preferred to quote from the Constitution on the Church to show how much the position of the laity is rooted in the very nature of the Church.

Lay Responsibility in Financial Affairs

There is no sign that the Council gave much consideration to lay participation in this area, apart from a fairly uninformative passage in the Decree on the Ministry and Life of Priests (21). However, when one considers the position of the laity as just described, it is impossible to exclude financial matters from the laity's sphere of responsibility. After all, money and property, donations and grants, are never an end in themselves for the Church, but always only a means for performing its real mission, coming to the aid of human beings in their need, as Jesus Christ did, to bring them, by word and deed, the love and life of God, and in all things to glorify God.[3]

As both past and present show, money and property are always both an opportunity and a danger for the Church. It is the opportunity to give appropriate and effective help to brothers in distress, to set up the institutions necessary for the life of the Church, to develop missionary work, to maintain schools and universities, to engage in adult education on a large scale—in short, to be present in the modern world.

On the other hand, it is the considerable danger of losing sight of the real goal, of neglecting the priority of the pastoral, of becoming a comfortable, rich Church, of obscuring the evangelical counsel of poverty, which applies no less to the Church as a whole than to individual Christians in the world. There is a great danger that a rich Church will lose credibility for its justified opposition to the welfare society.[4]

The way the Church handles donations, Church tax, grants and land, the way it behaves as an employer, the conditions on which it lets accommodation and the people to whom it lets it, the projects it supports or does not support in the third world, all this has a crucial effect on the credibility of its official preaching, and on the force of the lived testimony of all Christians. It is therefore totally impossible to make a sharp division between the theology of the nature of the Church and the Church's behaviour in economic and financial affairs; and it seems to me equally impossible to distinguish between a purely secular and a purely spiritual area in the Church.

The West German Joint Synod was therefore right to draw the conclusion, in its resolution already quoted, 'Responsibility of the Whole People of God for the Mission of the Church,' [5] that the responsibility of the laity on the various levels (parish, diocese, extra-diocesan affairs) must also include financial affairs.

The rôle of the laity in general

Many of the conciliar impulses have proved fruitful in West Germany. In many parishes an excellent partnership has become established between clergy and laity. In most dioceses, too, co-operation between bishops, priests and laity on the diocesan level is very good, if still capable of improvement in some details.

The parish councils, deanery and diocesan councils of laity (see the laity decree, 26), the diocesan pastoral councils (see *Christus Dominus*, 27) and the Central Committee of German Catholics have excellent, thoroughly discussed constitutions with detailed descriptions of their responsibilities. For supra-diocesan affairs, the Joint Synod voted to set up a unique instrument of co-operation, the 'Joint Conference' consisting of twelve members of the Bishops' Conference and twelve members of the Central Committee of German Catholics. The Conference's official tasks include the discussion of supra-diocesan tasks of the Church in West Germany which make demands both on the governing body (represented by the Bishops' Conference) and on the independent organizations (represented by the Central Committee).[6]

To deal with conflict between the authorities and the lay organizations in the various bodies, the constitutions include conflict-solving clauses. The Joint Synod went so far as to ask the pope, in a resolution adopted by an overwhelming majority, to confirm a detailed 'system of arbitration agencies and administrative courts for the dioceses in the Federal Republic of Germany.'[7] §31 of this document provides for authority to decide in disputes between clergy and Church bodies with which they have to work about denials of constitutional rights. However, the pope has not yet responded to this resolution of the Joint Synod.

Looking at this comprehensive structural provision for participation, one might think everything was ideal. Rules alone, however, are not enough. They may reduce conflicts by preventing them from developing and so help towards a fair settlement of those which do develop, but they do not create more vitality and creativity in the Church. Losses of efficiency due to friction (to borrow an image from engineering) are still often heavy because many priests and bishops fear—if only unconsciously—a loss of power or at least a restriction of it in areas which they feel to be essentially their own. And many of the laity feel that they are not taken seriously by priests and bishops. They often believe—and rarely without reason—that their advice is only reluctantly noted and in the end politely ignored. There is still a lot of mutual mistrust to be removed here.

In spite of all the constitutions, there is still uncertainty about the real spheres of responsibility of laity and clergy in the Church. Many bishops and priests regard the laity as welcome helpers in a period of a shortage of priests but do not inwardly accept the fundamental mission of the laity which was stressed by the Council. They tend to tie active laity to the clerical system, even conferring minor orders on them, or at least a commission in liturgical forms. This is matched by the tendency of a good many lay people to regard themselves as auxiliary clergy and so to avoid the uncertainties and difficulties of their independent Christian rôle in the world and the Church. The Catholic organizations (e.g., the Catholic Workers' Movement, the Catholic Women's League and the League of Catholic Youth) are beginning to grow again after a period of uncertainty caused by the creation of the councils. They too, however, occasionally come into conflict with the Church authorities. The superficial issue is quite often financial support, but underlying this is the tension between the autonomy of the organizations and their connection with the Church.[8]

Lay participation in financial affairs

On the parish level. The Joint Synod's recommendation was as follows: 'For the particular work of administering parochial assets and finances the parish council should set up a committee to draw up a budget according to pastoral criteria decided by the parish council, and to supervise its implementation.'[9] This recommendation has been put into practice or not depending on local Church regulations. In the diocese of Limburg, for example, the parish council elects the executive, which is the body responsible for financial administration. In the seven dioceses of Bavaria, on the other hand, such a system comes up against local Church regulations. Here the members of the administrative committee are elected directly by the parish; the parish priest is always the chairman. This means that elected lay people also have a share here in financial administration. There are, however, two independent bodies. The parish council decides on activities within the parish, but has no control over the necessary finances, while the administrative committee can determine financial (and so indirectly pastoral) priorities on its own. To reduce the effects of this duplication, which easily leads to conflict, the rules of the administrative committee stipulate [10] that a member of the committee should be invited to meetings of the parish council as a visitor, and that the chairman of the parish council should be invited to the administrative committee's meetings as a visitor. Before important decisions the administrative committee is also required to inform and consult the parish council in

good time. Before approving the draft budget, the administrative committee has to obtain the agreement of the parish council. If the two
sides are unable to agree, the committee's budget and the views of the
parish council are both submitted to higher ecclesiastical authority for
a decision.[11]

This corresponds for the most part with the Joint Synod's rules for
cases in which local Church regulations prevent independent decisions
by the parish council on financial matters. Nevertheless the situation as
described is unsatisfactory in that parishioners elect two bodies in
separate elections, and the two have partial competence for what is
essentially one organic process of decision-making. It is thus very regrettable that no steps have yet been taken to follow the Joint Synod's
call 'to seek changes in laws governing local Church regulations.' [12]

On the diocesan level. The Joint Synod rules: 'The work of administering the assets and finances of the Church is to be carried out by a
board of finance which takes independent decisions, guided by the
pastoral principles laid down by the diocesan pastoral council. It decides the budget and supervises its implementation.' [13] The description
of the responsibilities of the diocesan pastoral council includes: 'Determination of the pastoral principles governing the drawing up of the
budget.' [14]

The form of the financial committee which decides on the budget still
varies considerably in the different dioceses. The archdiocese of
Munich-Freising has a 'Diocesan Tax Committee' consisting of the
archbishop (chairman), the financial director (administrator of the cathedral and vice-chairman), three elected priests, nine elected lay
people and two members appointed by the archbishop. The nine lay
people are elected by the parish administrative committees.

The difficulty of this solution is that the electors hardly know the
candidates and that those elected have no further connection with the
electors and no formal link with the diocesan lay council or the pastoral
council. This is an obstacle to the free and continuous exchange of
information which is an essential condition for consultation and shared
responsibility.

For the future ways must be found to bring the bodies which advise
the archbishop into closer association with the Diocesan Tax Committee. This could be done by a change in election procedure. Nevertheless there have been in recent years remarkable efforts in this diocese
to involve the laity more actively. For some years now the draft budget
has been published, together with a report on the activities of the
previous year, so that everyone has access to the information. In addition, a member of the Diocesan Tax Committee has presented a de-

tailed report to a general meeting of the diocesan council of laity and listened to comment and criticism. On the occasion of the drawing up of the new budget, the vicar general and the financial director have had detailed consultations with the council of laity at which pastoral priorities and financial possibilities have been the main topics. The willingness to broaden the basis of lay participation even in financial affairs is unmistakable. Nevertheless it remains true that the many obligatory items of expenditure leave little scope for a real change in budgetary priorities. That, however, is not a problem of lay participation.

On the supra-diocesan level. The supra-diocesan budget, which is not inconsiderable in volume, is administered by the Association of German Dioceses, an independent legal entity. Because of the legal autonomy of this association (a union of the dioceses), the Joint Synod was only able to make recommendations for the revision of its constitution.[15] The effect of these recommendations would have been that the association's general council would have included one member elected by each diocesan pastoral council with advisory status (in addition to the bishop, as the voting member). The administrative committee would have been made up of the following voting members: one from each cathedral chapter, diocesan tax committee and diocesan pastoral council.[16] Since the administrative committee submits the draft budget to the general council, which then makes the final decision, this would have considerably improved lay participation in supra-diocesan affairs.

Unfortunately the association of dioceses, in the new constitution it adopted in 1977, accepted few of these recommendations. The fixed degree of lay participation was not extended. The diocesan bishop can now send an additional non-voting member to the administrative committee, and must appoint him in consultation with the diocesan pastoral council, but this is hardly more than a feeble echo of the Joint Synod's desire.

On the other hand, it must be regarded as a step forward that the 'Joint Conference' mentioned above, made up of representatives of the German Bishops' Conference and the Central Committee of German Catholics, includes on its agenda, under finance, a report from the president of the Bishops' Conference on the state of the Church in West Germany and the resulting priorities for the work of the association. The conference discusses this and produces suggestions for budgetary priorities.[17] This took place for the first time in 1977.

This procedure not only provides for lay participation in the form of intensive consultation; it also highlights the pastoral significance of church budgets.

SUMMARY AND FUTURE PROSPECTS

There are many moves in the right direction, if still very hesitant ones. Structures and constitutions—apart from that of the association of dioceses—are giving the laity considerable opportunities to extend their influence to financial affairs, though predominantly only in the form of advice. In practice, however, many misunderstandings still remain, and much mutual suspicion—a shameful situation among Christians.

Nevertheless it can be said that the pastoral significance of the Church's financial decisions is increasingly being recognized, and this probably owes something to the increased participation of the laity at the various levels.

There is an urgent need for more information for those who are supposed to advise, which will give their advice more weight; this will increase the willingness of those advised to accept the advice, which will encourage the advisers, which will increase trust.

This is the only way to put the present dispute about voting status or advisory status into perspective and avoid both excessive emphasis on votes cast without adequate information and insufficient attention to advice based on professional knowledge.

Given such intimate and trusting relations between bishops, priests and laity—in financial as in other matters—'a great many benefits' are indeed to be hoped for for the Church.

Translated by Francis McDonagh

Notes

1. Quoted from W. M. Abbott and J. Gallagher (ed.) *The Documents of Vatican II* (London & Baltimore, 1966): italics added.

2. Cited in future as 'Joint Synod: Participation.' The resolution is published in the official *Gesamtausgabe der Beschlüsse der Vollversammlung der Gemeinsamen Synode der Bistüer in der Bundesrepublik Deutschland,* vol. I (Freiburg, Basle & Vienna, 1976), cited as '*Synoden-Gesamtausgabe* I,' pp. 655ff. Cf. also the introduction by Wilhelm Pötter, loc. cit., pp. 637ff.

3. Cf. Joint Synod Resolution, 'The Pastoral Ministries in the Community,' *Synoden-Gesamtausgabe,* I, p. 603, 2.2.1.

4. See the Joint Synod's resolution 'Our Hope,' *Synoden-Gesamtausgabe,* I, p. 605.

5. Cf. above, n. 2. Relevant to this context: III, 1.3; 1.4; 1.16.3; 3.3.1 lit. d; 3.3.8; 3.3.10.3; 3.4.2 lit. e; IV, 3.1; 3.2 lit. c; 3.3 lit. b; 4.2.6; 4.2.1; 4.2.2; 4.2.7.

6. Loc. cit., IV, 3.1. and section 2 of the Joint Conference's agenda for 22 Nov 1976.

7. *Synoden-Gesamtausgabe*, I, pp. 734ff; cf. also the introduction by W. Bayerlein, loc. cit., pp. 727ff.

8. Cf. 'Joint Synod: Participation,' II, Nos 2, 4 and 7.

9. Loc. cit., III, 1.3.

10. Art. 27 of the constitution for parochial Church tax associations in the dioceses of Bavaria of 15 Sept 1971.

11. Loc. cit., Art. 29. para. 7.

12. 'Joint Synod: Participation,' III, 1.3.

13. Loc. cit., III, 3.3.10.3.

14. Loc. cit., III, 3.3.10.1 lit. d.

15. Loc. cit., IV, 4.2.

16. Loc. cit., IV, 4.2.2.

17. Item 2, para. 2, lit. d of the agenda of 22 November 1976.

Michel Brion

Care of Sick and Aged Clergy in France

THE total number of clergy [1] in France makes them a not inconsiderable social category, amounting to some 140,000. The budget for their own scheme of voluntary social security is considerable, too: 400 million francs, or 5,000 francs per annum for every cleric over 65. Theoretically based on individual contributions in order to conform to the law, the system is in fact dependent on contributions by religious bodies, according to their numbers. These bodies are free to levy a charge on their members or not, as they see fit, to pay for their contributions.

At present, the *Mutuelle Saint Martin* takes care of sick clergy (except in seven dioceses out of ninety, and 90,000 of the 100,000 religious); the *Caisse d'Allocations aux prêtres âgés* (CAPA) and the *Entraide des Missions et Instituts* (EMI) respectively of aged diocesan priests and religious. The sickness benefits are equivalent to those provided by the *Régime Général de Sécurité Sociale* (State social security), and the old-age pensions the same as the obligatory State minimum pension—5,500 francs. The national institutions developed progressively under pressure of social and political needs between 1950 and 1972. A new stage, brought on by similar pressures, will be created by the enforcement of the Law of 2 January 1978, creating the *Caisse Mutuelle d'Assurance maladie des Cultes* (mutual fund for sickness benefit for the clergy) and the *Caisse Mutuelle d'Assurance vieillesse des Cultes* (mutual fund for old-age benefits). These funds embrace all religions, whose personnel are not considered to be wage-earners in the meaning given to the term in social legislation. They stem from the new legal obligation for social protection imposed since 1978 on certain

96

fringe categories which had remained outside the scope of the social security legislation. In fact they take over the task of the voluntary organizations presently operating, with the only difference that they must also be open to the relatively few ministers of non-Catholic faiths.

FRENCH SOCIAL SECURITY

French social security rests on a patchwork of obligatory schemes, since the general scheme, so called because it was supposed to take over from all others after 1945, only embraces 64% of the population (82% of wage-earners), the rest being catered for by a number of other similar schemes, together with complementary schemes for both sickness and old age, the latter compulsory for wage-earners. This *imbroglio* has led to the institution of clearing houses to correct the fatal imbalance between social categories, both in the basic scheme (Law of 24 December 1974) and in the complementary schemes for wage-earners (Agreement of 8 December 1961), but French social security still remains strongly marked by a professional and mutual structure deriving from its origins, which has resisted the pressure for unification in 1945.

The French Church, as it existed in 1945-7, was unable to see the need to adhere to the unified structure the State sought to establish. It sided with those who contracted out and was freed from any obligation under the state scheme. Its clergy was too young and its institutions too powerful for it to foresee the rapid decline that was to affect its assets, establishments and resources, particularly after 1968, and face it with serious social security problems. Every 'incumbent' then lived modestly, but with no risks, with the religious body, whether diocese or congregation, to which he belonged, having a statutory obligation to see to his needs. This structure, in its pure state, was an embodiment of the canonical rules (Can. 981 and the vow of poverty) by which, as a counterpart to the cleric's commitment, he had a right to subsistence in the bosom of his community, both in sickness and in health.

The national bodies created in the years 1950-72 were in effect only clearing houses (on a demographic basis, since contributions are uniform and not related to the resources of different bodies) acting for the provident societies constituted by each religious body. The organization of their funds along the lines of social security funds changes nothing in this respect. Taken as a whole, the national organizations could be considered well-adapted to the French system of social security according to socio-professional groupings; their administrative structure by diocese and congregation forming two distinct sections and underlining the basic inspiration: that this is a specifically clerical undertaking.

AN AUTONOMOUS CLERICAL SCHEME: PROS AND CONS

The objections to the hierarchy's choice of an autonomous clerical scheme are based on two main considerations.

The oldest objection has come from clerics involved with the working classes, who cannot accept that the Church should adopt a position on the social security of its 'staff' that conflicts with the objectives of the workers' struggle, and without consultation with working class leaders. The evolution of French social security away from the unitary movement of 1945–7, has been influenced by conservative political forces, whereas the original movement sprang from the National Council of the Resistance, influenced by the Communist Party, which claims to be the 'party of the workers.' Hence the traditional opposition of the Left to any scheme based on social categories, which they see as an attack on social security and an attempt to dismantle its structure further, ending up with small mutual provident societies that would leave the way open for capitalist insurance. The clerics opposing the hierarchy's scheme have therefore taken up a stance of solidarity with the workers, although the attitude of the latter, helped by a strong current of self-interest, is more nuanced that it might seem, since one has to live with things as they are.

This solidarity goes hand in hand with a desire not to distinguish oneself from others as a cleric, but this objection has been more radically expressed by other groups who have questioned the whole concept of the status of a cleric as an aid to their argument. This point of view belongs mainly to religious who see their belonging to a religious body as a matter purely for their individual consciences, and one that should not affect their status as citizens. Modern practice of their teaching and charitable office has led many members of congregations to work out their vocations in an individual situation, which means taking paid work on an individual basis. There is considerable evidence that this has had a definite repercussion on their way of understanding and living the vow of poverty, which had previously seemed to consist in not disposing freely of one's assets, which in any case belonged to the community, whereas now they willingly hold on to their salary— which enables them to be personally generous—and send a proportion of it to their community as a contribution to its general expenses. Many see this as the final transformation of a religious congregation into a sort of secular institute. Perhaps the latter explains the former. In any case, and in more general terms, the diversity of tasks facing the Church, both laity and clergy, minister and militant, makes one tend to assimilate the two, to the extent of seeing the priest and religious as a sort of militant engaged in a specialist function, even if only temporarily. However, the social position of both should be the same and, as separate structures should be rejected, neither the maintenance of private schemes of social security nor particularist structures (congregations) recognized by the State can be justified. This view spells the death of the cleric working for his diocese or congregation and receiving everything from it in return.

A RADICAL EVOLUTION OF THE ACTIVITY OF THE CHURCH

A radical evolution of the activity of the Church and its clerics has to be recognized as a fact. I have shown elsewhere [2] how the Church in France has changed from a Church of religious institutions to a scattered Church whose committed members tend more and more to merge, without privileges, into the various institutions of secular life—which brings about a radical modification of the problem of their social security. This is now funded not by the religious community but by the occupational schemes operated by the professions in which they now work. It is a different world. Will this process continue? Undoubtedly. Will it be permanent? No one can tell, but all the signs are that it will not be reversed for a very long time. Seeing things calmly, however, one must recognize that this way of life is not yet by any means universal; many priests are still exclusively attached to the performance of their office in the traditional manner—a quite specific activity rewarded in France by the offerings of the faithful only—many priests and religious still carry out their tasks in the framework set by their communities, not to mention contemplatives and missionaries. The majority, as a final consideration, are old.

It also needs to be said that overall resources are declining as a result of this pastoral evolution, despite transfers that give a different impression. This unavoidable future and present situation call for the maintenance of a separate and slightly different social security scheme, at least as a transitional step, which is allowed by the French system, despite doctrinal objections, which leave room for compromise. However justifiable, theoretical arguments based on an idealistic view of social security and of the Church should stay in line with the realities of the situation.

THE PRESENT SITUATION

The problem, as I see it, was—and still is—to face up to the situation. Not a day passes without traditional Catholics denouncing the radical changes taking place in the Church, changes which, they claim, are replacing it with a different Church. They hold the bishops, led by 'officials' and 'theologians,' responsible for this state of affairs. While recognizing the facts, one cannot accept their point of view or join in the chorus of accusation. On this level, there is no denying that the Church is changing radically, and that those in their forties or fifties can hardly recognize the Church they were brought up in. Nor can it be denied that the hierarchy have brought about, or at least permitted, the course the Church is set on. Suffice to consider the pyramid (inverted) of the ages of the clergy, the considerable falling-off of religious observance among the young and the progressive laicization of Christian institutions to see that the Church will never be the same again—though it may be better.

In my view, whether this change is the result of a deliberate plan or reflects a more general change in society as a whole, or even represents a return to the early Church, those who have willed it or accepted it must accept its material consequences. Enterprises in decline, or in a process of regrouping or even liquidation, take care to preserve their personnel, particularly the older members, from the dramatic consequences of such changes. More generally, one has to recognize that any scheme of social protection through sharing out—including those based on professional categories!—must support itself by continued activity and a young base. Any lessening of activity, or progressive aging of personnel, ruin the scheme. This is what is happening to clerics: religious observance is falling off, their average age is increasing, and their younger members are increasingly moving into professional occupations, which provide a different source of social security. So we need to use another technique, as companies do when they go into liquidation, one that involves the use of capital—let us not fight shy of the word. This must then be *based on a sale of capital assets,* a corollary of the progressive abandonment of Christian institutions. Theoretically, this is the only possible solution.

However, those responsible have had the enormous good fortune that this evolution coincides with the decline of other social categories, such as agricultural workers and small traders. This phenomenon has forced the State to open a new clearing house to palliate the parallel decline in their pension funds, deprived of investors and loaded with beneficiaries. So all we have to do is go along with this process. Thanks to the law of 2 January 1978, the problem will be solved for the clergy in the same way: once the imbalance between old and young reaches a certain point, the State will make up the deficit in the pension fund.

The only trouble, pastorally speaking, was that this compensation was based only on a demographic base (as though one could not be old and rich!) and that therefore the wage-earners, who as a socio-professional category are numerous and young and therefore liable to bear the brunt of the cost—compensation being only provisionally incumbent on the State—rejected the principle through their trade union and political representatives. Despite its supposed working-class and Socialist bent, the Church in France had wanted to take advantage of the scheme. The contribution made by the State would have been considerable, though the individual, old-age pension would have been very small, which means one need not have too much of a complex about accepting it. But the Church has made a *faux pas,* as the vivid reaction of clerics engaged in pastoral work among the workers has made clear. Some would have wanted it, despite everything, to give a lordly demonstration of detachment and to study ways of making capital available to the same amount, a pastoral exercise in the first place rather than a financial one. Financial techniques could have been worked out later, such as the leaving grant made to farmers who left their farms to enable restructuring to be carried out. In any event, one has to learn how to hand things over when one can no longer take care of them oneself.

THE NEED FOR A SUPPLEMENTARY SCHEME

The support of the national body, however, is not going to be enough, for several reasons. As sickness benefit, because the national fund, which does not have the benefit of compensation and has to balance its income and expenditure, is in a few years going to be unable to pay its way owing to the increasing age of its constituents. As old-age benefit, because the meagre old-age pension [3] is going to need a supplementary fund set up, which again will have no assistance. So the problem is not solved and needs to be looked at again. Once again, *reconversion* is the key, uncovering basic problems which have unfortunately not been in the forefront of the argument, which has concentrated on structural problems. These basic problems are: the level of social security, for reasons already examined; internal solidarity between dioceses and congregations, and external solidarity with other social groups. These three problems have one common denominator: the extent of the financial resources of dioceses and congregations, appreciating that the exact level of individual remuneration of clerics dependent on their own religious bodies is of only limited interest.

However much it may vary, it is very little in relation to his work. In the traditional conception, a cleric is not rewarded in relation to the work he does, but only in relation to his basic needs, the fruit of his work going to benefit the body to which he belongs. This will have greater or lesser resources, often depending on investments it has been able to make in the past as a result of this sacrifice of individual means—the increased asset value of a well-situated building, for example. A seminary in the depths in the country may not be worth anything, and schools can be difficult to sell, but a disused seminary in a town is another matter, and schools or charitable institutions no longer needed in a city can raise six, ten, twenty million francs. So an inventory needs to be taken, especially of buildings no longer needed because of the change taking place. Often the work of the building can be kept on, usually on a private, secular basis, which changes its purpose, the purpose that was initially made possible by endless gifts, and particularly the dowries of thousands of nuns, which have founded it or maintained it. So we have no right to give the building up for nothing, without at least getting enough to assure the subsistence of those withdrawn from it. The concept of a leaving grant could again be useful here.

The only way for the French Church to face up to its obligations to the people it took on in a different climate is to appeal once more to the State without making a counter-balancing contribution. Some dioceses and congregations have realized this, but acted on their own without solidarity with the others. The problem is made worse by the fact that the system of social security henceforth in operation, though apparently satisfactory, weighs and will weigh heaviest on young bodies—by virtue of the equal contributions made by everyone under sixty-five—rather than on wealthy ones. A body most of whose members are over sixty-five will pay nothing and receive pensions to which it has made no contributions, while another, whose members are mostly young, will pay more than its share of contributions even if it is poor.[4] This is solidarity upside-down. Furthermore, there will be an unacceptable transfer of the canonical charge laid on the Bishop or Superior by virtue of a solemn contract.[5]

The only way is for all religious bodies to place all the capital they dispose of or could dispose of in a mutual fund for the benefit of their permanent members. To keep capital out of a mutual fund one has just set up,[6] on the financial pretext that capital and revenue should not be confused, makes no sense when an enterprise has to take the course of liquidating all or part of its activities. At this point, capital is always realized in order to acquit basic obligations. Since any scheme of adjudication would be impossible and the Church has practised the method of capitalization, without appreciating the fact, it must now operate it intelligently by realizing its capital, bearing in mind that its patrimony does not really belong to this or that congregation, but to the Church.[7] Once again, we need the courage to face up the requirements of a *reconversion,* and one that needs both preaching and practising.

Translated by Paul Burns

Notes

1. The word 'clergy' here includes: diocesan priests, male and female religious.

2. *Lumière et Vie* 129 (1976), pp. 17–19, 65–84.

3. In 1967, the French hierarchy set up a pension fund for retiring bishops with a monthly pension of 1,000 francs (plus mass stipends), the equivalent of 2,000 francs today.

4. The probable fact that the collective contribution—foreseen by the Law of 2 Jan. 1978—will be based on the number of old people for the sickness benefit contribution, and the number of wage-earners for the old-age pension contribution, only half solves the problem. The individual sickness contribution will be very high with a large number of old people, who impose a heavy burden on a sickness scheme. With the old-age pension, experience shows that the difficulties of getting the 'social assurees' to pay their contribution makes the schemes' treasurers reluctant to accept a high enough contribution on this score.

5. *Lumière et Vie* 129, 130, pp. 109–17.

6. The Assembly of the Bishops of France, in Nov. 1977, set up a Mutual Fund applicable to all the dioceses of France, designed to offset the disadvantage to dioceses with young personnel. It is based on a fixed contribution of 0.5% of all revenues. The religious congregations have made a similar provision among themselves. But these decisions do not solve the problem of the body—particularly a religious community—whose increasing age dries up its revenues, while its capital remains intact.

7. *Lumière et Vie* 129, 130, pp. 39–41.

Edward J. Kilmartin

Money and the Ministry
of the Sacraments

BELIEVE in Jesus Christ and be saved! A corollary to this basic message of the New Testament is affirmed in the story of Simon Magus reported in Acts 8:9–24: The power displayed by the apostolic imposition of hands is a 'gift of God' which cannot be bought 'with money.' Only the free response of faith is adequate to any form of bestowal of the Spirit.

Bishops and synods of the churches of the East and West have frequently condemned the 'simoniacal heresy.' They have also rejected practices which give even the appearance of simony. The history of canonical directives forbidding monetary or other offerings during the rites of ordination, baptism, penance and holy communion is notorious. In general this legislation was aimed not so much at curbing clerical greed as the avoidance of the scandal of simony.[1]

The ancient custom of offering gifts, in addition to bread and wine, before the eucharist (East) or anterior to the eucharistic prayer (Rome) presented no similar threat as long as the gifts were delivered to the bishop for distribution. In the West, at least, the direct appropriation of gifts by the priest met with some resistance. But at the time when this practice was becoming more acceptable in the early Middle Ages another western mode of offering emerged which provoked a more enduring and unfavourable response from the Roman Church.

THE GENESIS AND MEDIEVAL INTERPRETATION OF THE MASS STIPEND

This new form of offering for the eucharist originated in the churches of the West influenced not only by Old Testament models of sacrifice and priesthood but also by eastern liturgical practices and a German legal understanding of gift. Here the eucharistic sacrifice was seen as an indissoluble whole offered by the Church through the priest who acted as mediator between God and the people. Under eastern influence the laity traditionally offered gifts before the eucharist which were reckoned as a sacrifice of almsgiving 'for God' to be used by the Church. In the liturgy the priest brought these gifts before God as representative of the donor. And even when the Roman custom of presenting gifts during mass began to be imitated, the action was not interpreted according to the old Roman way as a co-offering of the mass.

In this milieu offerings were valued as a means of associating the donor in a more intimate way with the sacrifice on the side of the priest. It enabled him to share in the blessings of the mass in a fuller way than other participants. This latter notion fostered the conviction that it is more advantageous to be the only donor of a gift for the mass. When this was coupled with the German legal understanding of a gift it led to the view that the mass is a proper spiritual return from the priest who appropriated the gift for his use. For in contemporary German law it belonged to the essence of a gift that it be sealed as unreturnable by a remuneration.

The practice of offering a gift before or during mass with the understanding that the priest is obliged to offer it to the exclusion of other gifts is characteristic of the mass stipend. An exact date of the origin of this practice cannot be determined. It is first found in Gaul, West Gothic Spain, the British Isles and France. By the beginning of the ninth century it had become so widespread in Italy that it commanded the attention of the Roman Synod of 826 AD, under Pope Eugene II.[2] The custom was rejected by the synod. It prohibits the priest from refusing to accept the gifts of all. No appeal is made to the original meaning of the offertory procession, nor is any reference made to the Roman legal principle of free donation without recompense. Rather, the synod argues that this style of offering is based on a misunderstanding of the priest's mediatorial rôle: the priest is mediator for all! However, while accepting the Old Testament concept of the priest as a mediator between God and mankind, the synod clings to the old Roman view that the eucharist is a sign of the unity of the Church and the people truly co-operators in the celebration.

Despite the continuing uneasiness of the Roman Church and its theologians, this form of offering eventually took hold everywhere in the West. By the beginning of the thirteenth century it was firmly established and the procedure defined so as to correspond to the demands of Roman law for exactitude in legally significant proceedings and relations. During the same century scholastic theology supplied three key elements for what was to become the common Catholic theological interpretation of the mass stipend: [3]

1. The Church approves the practice of allowing priests to accept the gift of one to the exclusion of others and obliges him to do so when he agrees to offer the mass *in solidum* for one donor. Hence there must be blessings derived from the mass *ex opere operato,* i.e., independently of the devotion of those actually present. Moreover, these fruits must be limited both intensively and extensively and are shared according to the capacity of the recipients;

2. The priest has the power to consecrate the bread and wine and so he also has authority over these fruits. He can determine by an act of his will the application of the fruits derived *ex opere operato* from the mass which are distinguished from those which come to the priest as celebrant and to the church at large; and finally,

3. The offering of a gift to obtain the special fruit which the priest can apply is not simoniacal. It is a free will contribution to the livelihood of the priest (Thomas Aquinas) or an alms (John Duns Scotus).

Since the magisterium of the West relied in increasing measure on scientific theology from this period onward, the interpretation of the schools became the official position of the Roman Catholic Church. In our day however this theology has been subjected to severe criticism by Catholic theologians. As a consequence its very core has been removed even in official teaching of the Catholic Church.

THE MODERN INTERPRETATION OF THE MASS STIPEND

A new approach to the theology of the mass stipend was proposed by Karl Rahner almost three decades ago. Initially it met with some opposition but now holds the field. This view excludes the concept of fruits derived from the mass *ex opere operato* and so the ability of the priest to apply any special fruit to the donor of a gift. It is only the devotion of those actually involved in the offering of the mass through their physical presence which measures the effects which the actual offering has on them and the blessings extended to those for whom they offer. The stipend is an expression of the devotion of the donor. Only in this sense can it be the occasion for the bestowal of blessings on the donor and those for whom he prays. The devotion attached to the offering of the gift may well increase, and so the fruits, when the donor is present at the mass for which he made an offering. Still these fruits are not increased by the simple fact that the gift is assigned to a particular mass. Only the devotion of those physically present at the mass can be the occasion for this increase.[4]

This explanation which concentrates on the spiritual character of the stipend had led Catholic scholars to interpret it as a constitutive sign of the integration of the donor into the eucharistic worship—to relate it to the old offertory procession.

An abortive nineteenth-century attempt was made in this direction by an anonymous author who interpreted the stipend as a means of uniting the donor with the mass as was formerly done through the offertory procession.[5] In this century the German canonist Klaus Mörsdorf espoused this thesis.[6] He concluded that the essential purpose of the stipend is to bring the donor into a special relation to the sacrifice of the Mass just as in the case of the offertory procession. As such, it can only be accepted by or from one who has the right to participate in the mass. Though given outside mass it is ordered to the sacrificial offering by the priest who acts as representative of the donor. After the application it comes to the priest as public servant of the Church.

Recently this explanation has found additional support in the historical study of one of Mörsdorf's students, Adalbert Mayer. Through his investigation of the origin and reasons for the establishment of the mass stipend, he is able to conclude that it must be interpreted along the lines of the old Roman offertory procession.[7]

The apostolic letter of Paul VI, *Firma in traditione* (15 June, 1974) shows the influence of this theological consensus. In this document, which grants new faculties for dealing with problems connected with mass stipends, he briefly summarizes his understanding of the practice. It is a form of sacrifice of almsgiving added to the eucharistic sacrifice. Through it the faithful are enabled to participate more intimately in the mass and contribute to the needs of the Church and its ministers. It is a 'sign of the union of the baptized person with Christ and of the faithful with the priest who exercises his ministry for their good.' [8]

RELATION BETWEEN STIPEND AND OFFERTORY PROCESSION

While there is general agreement among Catholic scholars that the stipend is a form of integration into the mass, the precise relationship between the stipend and the old offertory procession is interpreted in different ways, for the theology of the role of priest and laity which seems to undergird the old Roman offertory procession is not always accepted.

The offerings of the people had great significance in the old Roman liturgy. This is rather surprising since this liturgy is noted for its lack of rich symbolism, care to omit superfluous rites and for its juridical, rather than symbolic language. Hence one should be inclined to interpret the offering of gifts not only as a symbolic action but as 'a legally understood cooperation of all participants in the worship.' [9]

Here the priest appears to exercise a pastoral office which includes liturgical leadership as one of its functions. The Roman ordination rites of presbyters during the first millenium also indicate that the presbyter is given a share in a pastoral office which qualifies him for liturgical leadership. Within this liturgical theology the priest seems to be required for the celebration of the eucharist not because of a power of consecration which makes him a direct representative of Christ independently of his ecclesial relationship but because pastoral office is a constitutive element of the sacramental structure of the Church. [10] Since the Church most perfectly manifests and realizes itself in the eucharist the presence of this essential element of the structure of church is required.

The content of the Roman eucharistic prayer is consistent with this outlook. It is an act of faith of the whole community and the 'form' of the ritual action which includes the offertory procession. The structure of this prayer cannot be easily reconciled with a narrow theology of 'moment of consecration.' It contains a petition for consecration after the account of institution which is comparable to the Spirit epiclesis of the East. [11] The *Supplices te rogamus* of the Roman canon asks that the bread and wine be brought 'by the hands of your holy angel' to the heavenly altar 'in order that we who receive your Son's most holy body and blood at this altar here' may be sanctified.

In this liturgical theology the priest emerges as the representative of the faith of the Church at the level of the rite. His activity connotes the active presence of Christ the head of the Church who, with the Spirit, is the ultimate source of this act of faith of the worshipping community. The priest represents Christ by representing the Church and represents the Church by representing Christ. This reciprocal relation is possible because the minister directly represents the eucharistic faith of the community and so serves as transparency for Christ who, together with the Spirit, is the grounds for this acceptable act of sacrifice of praise made by the Church. [12] Consequently the offertory procession is a symbolic expression of the integration of the donor into the prayer of sacrifice of praise which the priest pronounces in the name of all. It signifies the real co-offering of the participants on the level of the eucharistic rite.

In this conception of the eucharistic celebration, stress is placed on the individual prayers and actions which are gathered by the priest to form one meaning. The eucharist is not considered to be a unified sacrificial act accomplished by the priest independently of, and at the same time in the name of the people. Eventually, under the influence of Old Testament models, the eucharistic sacrifice was interpreted as an indissoluble whole accomplished by the priest as a mediator between God and the people. This interpretation was embraced by Rome in the Middle Ages and has continued to influence Roman Catholic theology down to modern times.

A variation of this theology, which underscores the relation between the priest and Christ, is found in Piux XII's encyclical letter, *Mediator Dei* and is repeated in II Vatican's *Lumen Gentium,* no. 10: 'Acting in the person of Christ, he [the priest] brings about the eucharistic sacrifice and offers it to God in the name of the people. For their part, the faithful join in the offering of the eucharist in virtue of their royal priesthood.' [13] The ritual offering of the sacrifice of Christ is thus identified, as in *Mediator Dei,* [14] with the 'unbloody immolation' occurring at the recitation of the account of institution of the eucharist. The priest, in virtue of the power of orders, functions as direct representative of Christ independently of his function to represent the people.

Paul VI operates out of this theology when he stresses that the primary goal of the offering of a stipend is to unite the donor 'more closely with Christ himself as victim,' and when he says that the faithful 'add to it [eucharistic sacrifice] a form of sacrifice of their own.' He relates the stipend to an aspect of the old Roman offertory procession but does not embrace the theological understanding of the role of priest and people which it expresses.

More recent studies by Catholic theologians and liturgiologists on the theology of the mass and priesthood show a preference for the understanding of the dynamics of the eucharistic celebration which seems to underlie the old offertory procession. However the scholastic theology of the eucharistic sacrifice represented in the official Roman Catholic position also finds support among modern Catholic scholars. Still there is one important point of agreement on both sides: The proper meaning of the stipend does not lie in the material sphere and, in the present pastoral situation, there is a real need to emphasize its religious significance.

THE ENDURING VALUE OF AN ANCIENT CUSTOM

The current practice of making offerings for masses with no intention of being liturgically present is surely not ideal. In whatever way one interprets the gift as expression of spiritual integration into the eucharistic sacrifice, but especially in the old Roman perspective, it is appropriate for the donor to be physically present. Only in this way can his devotion, which is expressed by the gift, be fully integrated into the liturgical sacrifice of praise. Also the custom whereby the priest retains the gift for his exclusive use, when his support is otherwise adequately provided for, is an anomaly. The canonical directive: stipend excludes stipend, forestalls further abuses. But if the offerings are really used for 'the needs of the Church' this restriction becomes anachronistic.

With all its limitations however the mass stipend has preserved a custom which, if properly interpreted and practiced, should be retained. In the eucharist the community is invited to unite itself to the worship of Christ by which he consecrated himself to God 'on behalf of the many.' Motivated by this invitation it is fitting that the participants express the consecration of self by offering the fruits of their daily work. This symbolic gesture corresponds to the goal of the eucharist which is expressed in the new offertory prayer. The bread and wine are called fruit of the earth and the 'work of human hands.' Inserted into the memorial of the sacrifice of Christ they symbolize the consecration of the material world and all human endeavour to God. The use of the offering for the needs of the Church and world is also proper. It should not be discarded! True service of God always involves the service of mankind.

Offerings made for the eucharist will help to build up the Church as a 'spiritual temple' in the measure that the donor, as well as the priest who receives the gift from the altar, employ it as expression of a priestly vocation. Through the gift the donor should give cultic expression to his priestly service of God and mankind. The priest who receives the gift from the altar should, in turn, exercise this same priesthood by using it to witness to God's love for those in need. In this way both the donor and the priest answer the summons of the gospel to live the whole of life as a cultic act: 'Come to him, to the living stone . . . and like living stones be yourselves built up into a spiritual house, to be a holy priesthood, to offer spiritual sacrifices acceptable to God through Jesus Christ' (1 Pt 2:4–5).

Notes

1. Cn 48 of the Spanish Council of Elvira (circa 306 AD) provides the earliest example of such legislation. It forbids offerings of money during baptism because of the appearance of simony. J. Vives, *Concilios Visigóthicos e Hispano-Romanos* (Barcelona, 1963), p. 10.

2. Cn 17 (*Monumenta Germaniae Historia:* Capitularia regum Francorum I, ed. A. Boretius (Leipzig, ²1960), p. 374.

3. E. J. Kilmartin, 'The One Fruit and the Many Fruits of the Mass,' *Proceedings of the Catholic Theological Society of America,* p. 21 (1966), pp. 43–52.

4. K. Rahner, 'Die vielen Messen und das eine Opfer,' *Zeitschrift für katholische Theologie* 71 (1949), pp. 307–15.

5. 'Ueber den Gebrauch der Messstipendiums,' *Theologischpraktische Monatschrift* 2/1 (1828), p. 392.

6. 'Erwägungen zum Begriff und zur Rechtfertigung des Messstipendiums,' *Theologie in Geschichte und Gegenwart,* ed. J. Auer and H. Volk (Munich, 1957), pp. 103–22.

7. *Triebkräfte und Grundlinien der Entstehung des Messstipendiums* (Münchener Theologische Studien III. Kanonische Abteilung 34) (St Ottilien 1976), pp. 270–71.

8. A. Flannery, *Vatican II: The Conciliar and Post Conciliar Documents* (Collegeville, 1975), p. 277.

9. Mayer, op. cit., p. 74.

10. H. J. Schulz, 'Die Grundlinien der kirchlichen Amtes im Spiegel der Eucharistiefeier und der Ordinationsliturgie des Römischen und des Byzantinischen Ritus,' *Cattolica* 29 (1975), pp. 325–40.

11. E. J. Kilmartin, 'Sacrificium Laudis,' *Theological Studies* 35 (1974), pp. 285–87.

12. E. J. Kilmartin, 'Apostolic Office: Sacrament of Christ,' *Theological Studies* 36 (1975), pp. 250, 254–60.

13. Flannery, op. cit., p. 361.

14. *Acta Apostolicae Sedis* 39 (1974), pp. 555–56.

PART III

Bulletins

Jacques Schmitz

The Co-existence of Church and Socialist State in Poland

FROM COMPETITION TO CO-EXISTENCE

IT WAS a very special visit that the Secretary-General of the United Workers' Party of Poland (PUWP), Edward Gierek, made in December last year to Pope Paul VI during his Italian journey. This was not because it was so unique in relationships between the Vatican and the socialist countries of Eastern Europe. One of the consequences of the *Ostpolitik* initiated by his predecessor, John XXIII, Pope Paul received leaders of the Eastern European countries such as Andrei Gromyko (Soviet Foreign Minister), Podgorny (who was then President of the Soviet Union), Josip Broz Tito (President of Yugoslavia) and several other leaders of Eastern Bloc countries—Ceausescu (Romania), Kadar (Hungary) and Zhivkov (Bulgaria).

The significance of Gierek's visit to the pope is to be found above all in the special nature of the relationship between the Polish state and the Roman Catholic Church in Poland. More than in any other Socialist country, the Polish Church is able to rely on the great majority of the people and relationships between Church and State have been marked by irreconcilable conflict, a struggle that has continued for decades. On the one hand, there is the PUWP, which claims to lead the Polish nation politically and economically and regards itself as responsible for carrying out the historical task of the Polish working class, that is, the task of constructing a qualitatively new social system, Socialism. On the other hand, there is the Roman Catholic Church, which makes almost as great claims to leadership, a leadership that is not limited to purely spiritual and moral questions.

The Vatican reception of Gierek marked a temporary peak in the détente between Rome and the Socialist countries of Eastern Europe in general and between the PUWP and the Polish primate, Cardinal Stefan Wyczyński in particular. A process of détente had been gradually taking place after the confrontations in the nineteen-fifties and sixties when the party leader Gomulka was succeeded by Edward Gierek after the violent quarrels of December 1970. Although the air had not been completely freed of smoke from the shooting, relationships between Church and State had become much more normal. As a leading Polish journalist and party-member, Miroslaw Wojciechowski said last year in an interview with the Dutch national newspaper, the *Volkskrant,* 'Although we would not call it by that name, we in Poland have brought about a historical compromise. An authentic compromise in which concessions have been made on both sides.'

There is a clear analogy with the aims of the Italian Communist Party (PCI). The PCI is hoping to collaborate with Christians and the Italian Christian Democratic Party and, like the PUWP, is trying to do this on the basis of an analysis of the power structures in society. In the opinion of both parties, certain aspects of the Christian world are regarded as (at least potentially) progressive forces and therefore as allies in the struggle for a better society. But, whereas in Italy the PCI is a factor of growing strength forcing the Christian Democrats to make compromises, in Poland the powerful colossus of the Roman Catholic Church is the omnipresent factor with which the State and the Communist leaders have to reckon at all times.

Ever since the Communists and the Socialists of Poland, united in the one PUWP, had begun to work for a socialist State after the war, the Roman Catholic Church set itself up as the most important political opposition to the new power. Each side persisted obstinately in its own expectations of the future and these were diametrically opposed. In the years following the war, the Communists were convinced that the population of Poland would become more and more secularized and the Church would become less and less influential as Socialism gained ground. The Church leaders, on the other hand, did not believe that Socialism would last long and were convinced that it would collapse quite soon as a result of internal conflict and external pressure. Both Church and State tried to hasten the process that each wanted and expected to take place and were, as a result, for years at daggers drawn.

One of the consequences of the changed structure of the population in the People's Republic of Poland was that the Catholic population increased until it reached 90% of the total population (in the 1930 census, it was only 75%). This does not mean that all these Catholics are practising members of the Church. A shortage of statistical information forced those responsible for recent statistics to rely on baptismal lists and these are never reliable sources of information of this kind. It is, however, possible to say that the majority of Poles are in one way or another rooted in Roman Catholicism and that the Church in this way has a strong influence, mainly a moral one, on public and private life in the People's Republic. The Church still relies on by far the greater part of the population and is able to exert a strong spiritual influence especially on the frequently conservative non-urban population, although its influence is not confined solely to the rural districts.

When the Communists and Socialists came to power in 1944–1945, they at first took this religious and social influence of the Church very seriously. The Manifesto of Lublin (22 July 1944) guaranteed, among other things, the freedom of conscience and rights of the Catholic Church and its members. About a year later, however, the government of national unity put an end to the 1925 Concordat, with the result that the legal position of the largest church community in Poland and its relationship with the State were no longer regulated. There was a normative vacuum that formed the basis for a series of conflicts which could not be prevented by the treaty concluded after lengthy negotiations in 1950 by the Polish bishops and the government. Between 1952 and 1955, the latent struggle between the two powers became much more open and the State tried very hard to banish the Church from public life. Seminaries and Catholic faculties at the Polish universities were closed, members at all levels of the Catholic hierarchy were placed in custody or confinement (as was, for example, Cardinal Wyczyński in 1953) and it was not until 1956 that there was any sign of a thaw in the attitude of the State authorities.

In May 1957, the new party leader Gomulka declared that he recognized the need for co-existence between believers and non-believers, the Church and Socialists, the Church hierarchy and the proletarian power. The increased latitude was exploited by the Roman Catholic Church, however, which, from 1957 onwards, tried to strengthen its own position in Poland. In this context, it is important to note that the year 966 is regarded in Poland as the year when the Polish nation began its existence. It is also the date when King Mieszko I and the whole of his court were converted to Christianity. On the thousandth anniversary of this date, the Millennium Poloniae, in 1966, the Church disputed, openly and for the last time, the national identity and political legality of the Communist government. The climax of this confrontation was reached when the Church celebrated the anniversary separately from the State.

Since then, a mutual recognition of each other's right to live has gradually and through force of circumstances come about. The Church has come to see that the Socialist State is permanent and more and more believers have also come to recognize the value of many of the government's achievements and the social perspective revealed by Socialism. On the other hand, the Party and the State have also come to accept the ideological power exercised by the Church and have worked towards détente and collaboration with the religious authorities. This is partly, of course, because it has proved impossible for the State to solve the pressing political and economic problems without the support of the Roman Catholic Church. As Janusz Stefanowicz, the editor in chief of the Catholic daily newspaper *Slowo Powszechne* ('Universal Word') has often pointed out, the historical roots of Roman Catholicism in Poland are deep and ineradicable and 'even the most convinced atheist is bound to admit that, in a thousand years of Polish independence, the Church has become an inseparable part of the nation's identity, continuity and culture. I would go further and say that recent history has shown that Socialism, even though it has attracted millions of believers with its social programme, has not succeeded in creating a uniform atheistic society.'

It was with a certain pride that the Cracow weekly paper *Tygodnik Powszechny* ('Universal Weekly') confirmed Stefanowicz' opinion at the beginning of this year with a series of figures. On 20 October 1977, this newspaper claims, there were 19,865 priests in Poland, 15,067 seculars and 5,798 religious. It is of interest to reproduce a part of the information published about the number of those in seminaries and recently ordained:

SEMINARIANS

Year	total	diocesan	religious orders
1971	4088	3097	991
1972	4130	3057	1073
1973	4174	3035	1139
1974	4216	3091	1125
1975	4385	3120	1265
1976	4705	3410	1295
1977	5058	3607	1451

RECENTLY ORDAINED PRIESTS

Year	total	diocesan	religious orders
1971	480	356	124
1972	604	471	133
1973	557	450	107
1974	638	486	152
1975	606	455	151
1976	477	319	158
1977	438	341	97

THE STRENGTH OF THE PEOPLE'S CHURCH

Although the Polish Church is no longer openly opposed to the State, it cannot be said that it is in any sense friendly towards it. In Poland, Catholicism has always been and still is on average conservative and only a handful of higher ranking religious leaders are to some extent positive in their attitude towards the government. The Church has always been traditional. There is a strongly traditional cult of Mary, for example, and hardly any trace of a progressive theological movement as elsewhere in the Catholic Church today. The Polish hierarchy does not in any way feel impelled to renew itself theologically or liturgically. The churches are packed every Sunday, with many young people in the congregations, and anyone who wants to enter a seminary or a religious community may have to put his or her name on a waiting list (this is an almost unknown luxury in most national churches in the West today).

In *Le Monde Diplomatique* of March 1978, Jean Offredo called Polish Catholicism a mass religion, a patriotic religion and a Marial and clerical Christian phenomenon. This description is more or less complete. The mass participation in religious life that characterizes Polish Catholicism makes it almost a true people's religion, which, despite the impulses of the liberal Catholic movement that is certainly present in Poland (groups of Catholic intellectuals, journals such as *Znak, Wiez* and *Tygodnik Powszechny* and so on), is firmly based on a strong hierarchy and an exceptional faithfulness to tradition.

Polish Catholicism is also intensely patriotic and this comes from the special place that the Church has always occupied in the thousand years of Polish national history. The Church has always been a binding force in the difficult periods of Polish history, such a strong binding force indeed that the equation Polish = Catholic is certainly not exaggerated. Poland has almost continuously been threatened from outside, trampled underfoot, squeezed between three other greater powers (Orthodox Russia, Lutheran Prussia and Catholic Austria) and for a long time it was a 'nation without a state.' In such times of stress and threat, Polish nationality was able to continue within the Church.

It is important to mention, if only briefly, the great power and influence and the high status of the clergy in Poland. The priest is respected in an almost old-fashioned way in Poland and the priesthood is still the only guide through whom the truth can be known.

Our picture of the Polish Church would not be complete without an outline of the part that it plays in politics. Because it is a mass religion and has a very strong leadership, it is a very important factor in society and politics, although not at parliamentary level. In the Sejm (the Polish parliament), twelve of the four hundred and sixty representatives are Catholics who belong to no party, but to one of three groupings. Five of these Catholic members of the Sejm are representatives of Znak ('Sign'), five are representatives of the Pax movement and two are representatives of the Christian-Social Union (CSS).

Up to the present, the Znak group has itself decided who should represent it in the Sejm. At the last election, however, the State wanted to have a greater influence on the nominations. Stanislaw Stomma, the leader of Znak, and his supporters in Cracow opposed this and refused to sit in the Sejm. Others, who were more sympathetic towards Socialism, allowed themselves to be nominated as candidates, partly in order not to endanger the Znak representation in the Sejm. This political or rather tactical problem has led to a deep internal disagreement, which is still far from being resolved.

Konstantin Lubienski of Znak and Boleslaw Piasecki of Pax are members of the Council of State. Each of the three groups is different from the others in its attitude towards Socialism, but none opposes the new Socialist order. Each group tries in its own way to further the specific interests of the Church and its members in the Polish parliament.

The Catholic voice is not only heard in the Sejm. There are also more than fifty newspapers and periodicals published by Catholic organizations in Poland. There are also seventeen Catholic book publishers, including the scientific publishing house of the Catholic University of Lublin, which is the only remaining Catholic university in Eastern Europe.

The Church is regularly involved in political questions, although often indirectly, sometimes of its own accord and sometimes at the request, as it were, of the government. The PUWP had, for example, to tone down a number of proposed revisions of the Polish constitution in 1976 because of pressure from the Polish bishops. These were principally passages about the 'leading part played by the Party in the State' and Poland's 'unbreakable fraternal solidarity with the Soviet Union.' The Church was, however, directly involved in the serious troubles that occurred as a result of the sudden sharp rise in food prices in the summer of 1976. One of the worst effects of the announcement of higher prices was protest on the part of workers, especially in Radom and Ursus and Premier Pjotr Jaroszewicz was forced to withdraw the government's decision to raise prices on the evening of the announcement. After the scenes and demonstrations, Cardinal Wyczyński sent a letter, six pages long, signed by himself and the secretariat of the Polish episcopate, to Premier Jaroszewicz, supporting the 'honest' workers and the members of the committee created to defend the workers (KOR) who found themselves in prison after the demonstrations. The Conference of the Polish Episcopate made a critical analysis of the government's intervention in the price manoeuvres in June 1976 (9 August 1976). The members of the Conference also showed that they understood the complex nature of the situation and called on Catholics to 'increase their commitment and to work honestly' and to be 'ready to make sacrifices in the general interest and to maintain the social order.'

This incident gives a good idea of the critical distance and the co-responsibility of the Polish Church. In the knowledge that the political and economic problems of Poland cannot be solved by the government alone without the support of the Church leaders, Cardinal Wyczyński clearly hopes that his constructive contribution will result in greater religious freedom. He has several times stressed, round about the end of last year and the beginning of this, that the Church is responsible for morality and that 'it is necessary for men to overcome the mistaken idea that there is no connection between economic life and Christian morality.' In this way, the Church is urged by the State to call for better and increased production and to improve the morality of the workers, so that the country will eventually be able to overcome its economic difficulties.

Cardinal Wyczyński has on several occasions emphasized that the Church is not demanding to have a greater influence on state affairs in return for this support. In December last year, for instance, he declared that 'the Church is not demanding the right to govern the material order in this world or to exercise authority over the economy.' A month later, he said almost the same thing again: 'The Church is more intent on collaborating with the State than on opposing it openly, because its freedom of movement depends on a harmonious relationship with the Communist authorities. This is why the Church does not give enthusiastic support to what such dissident intellectuals as the members of the KOR are doing.' As the Polish journalist Wojciechowski has said, 'the Church works parallel to the KOR, but does not consult with it and is always a step or two behind. The Church makes use of the situation in order to regulate some of her own affairs more quickly, but does not want anyone to take the wind out of her sails. Cardinal Wyczyński monopolizes the opposition and will not let that position be taken from him.'

As long as it remains within his power, the relationship will continue to be 'harmonious.' But he is an old man and it is rumoured that he is suffering from a serious illness. Whether this is true or not, he will certainly have to give way to another. The next primate of Poland will have to tone down his militant attitude or else lose all influence. It has become clear over the past thirty or so years that a militant anti-Communism has not produced positive results either for the Church or for the Polish nation.

Translated by David Smith

Photios Nikitopoulos

The Survival of the Orthodox Churches
of the Near East

STARTING-POINT

THE political and geographical area known as the Near or Middle East lies on the eastern side of the Adriatic, and is generally taken to include the Balkan countries and those that give on to the eastern and south-eastern shores of the Mediterranean. The area has always been of particular interest to church historians, and rightly so, since it was the cradle of Christianity, and has an extraordinary history, through which the local Orthodox Churches of the first seven Ecumenical Councils have somehow survived. These are: the ancient Patriarchates of Constantinople, Alexandria, Antioch and Jerusalem, the Archbishopric of Cyprus, and the later 'national' Churches of Greece, Serbia, Rumania, Bulgaria and, finally, Albania.

The last great common crisis they had to face was subjection to the Turkish yoke. This was followed by the great historical realignments of the nineteenth and twentieth centuries, which are still having their repercussions today. It was in fact the collapse of Turkish domination that gave rise to the formation of the different national States of the Balkans and the consequent formation of their respective Churches, withdrawn from the jurisdiction of the Church of Constantinople, which was to remain prisoner to a hostile regime and victim of the intolerant fanaticism of Turkey. Another victim of this hostility was the Patriarchate of Antioch, forced to seek refuge outside the confines of Turkey, which was itself then subjected to the colonizing forces of the

European powers, which also embraced all the rest of the Churches under discussion. The end of colonialism brought about a situation that naturally affected the Churches in their respective territories. The Communist take-over of the Balkan countries, with the exception of Greece, then faced the Churches with a new experience and new problems.

All this presents the Orthodox Churches of the Near East with a *challenge:* how to survive in the new scheme of things obtaining in the world they find themselves in, without themselves 'being of this world' (Jn. 18: 36). Adaptation to a whole complex of factors established by the new historical situation is a necessity, but so is remaining true to their own nature. In other words, while living in this century, they must not model themselves on the behaviour of the world around them (Rom. 12: 2), and must seek to impose their spiritual tradition harmoniously on the new structures of life. In fact, this is what has happened.

THE PRESENT SITUATION

Taking each Church in turn, I propose to give an account, necessarily summary, of the present-day situation of the Orthodox Churches of the Near East.

The Ecumenical Patriarchate of Constantinople

The elimination of the Greek population from Asia Minor and Eastern Thrace, resulting from the unhappy outcome of the Graeco-Turkish encounter of 1919–22, deprived the Church of Constantinople of nearly all its dioceses in those territories. At the same time, the new situation produced by the coming of Kemal Ataturk and the founding of the Turkish Republic in 1923 changed the status of the Ecumenical Patriarchate (Lausanne Agreement, 1923); the privileges accorded to it by the Sultan were abolished; since then it has not in practice been able to enjoy the religious freedom declared by the Turkish State; it lives today in an atmosphere of hostile toleration, if not of outright persecution.

The Cyprus question had unfavourable effects on the Greek Orthodox population of Constantinople, who were made victims of a deliberate policy of revenge by the Turks. A reign of terror was imposed: the vandalism of 1955, with kidnappings, bomb attacks, and so on, has led to a climate of fear and distrust that amounts to an undeclared persecution, which has led the Greek Orthodox to seek refuge in Greece and other free countries. This has been a real exodus.[1] Communities and parishes, once flourishing, with splendid schools and other institutions, have been scattered to the winds. The theological faculty of *Calche* was forcibly closed; the patriarchal printing works was shut down; ecclesiastical goods were seized under various pretexts; certain bishops were forbidden to travel outside Turkey; the agreement to have the patriarchal palace, which had been destroyed in a fire, rebuilt, was cancelled. These are the conditions under which the Church of Constantinople lives: a Church imprisoned, or, if one prefers, in a state of seige, forced to exist partly in the open and partly hidden. This material impoverishment, however, is made up for by a wonderful spiritual influence and the pre-eminence it still enjoys in the Orthodox world. Its initiatives in the ecumenical field are proof of this. It remains a treasure-house of prudence and wisdom, the heart and mind of Orthodoxy.

Physically, however, it is now made up mainly of dioceses outside Turkey: in Greece (Crete, the Dodecanese and Mount Athos), in the rest of Europe, America, Oceania (where its jurisdiction was extended by virtue of Canon 28 of the Fourth Ecumenical Council), with a total of 2,000 parishes and one hundred monasteries. The existence of this free part is enough to sustain the beseiged and beleaguered Patriarchate, spiritually, morally and economically.

The Patriarchate of Alexandria

The jurisdiction of the Patriarchate extends over the whole of Africa, but from the time of the Early Church the Greek community in Egypt formed its chief constituency. Recently, Nasser's policies against the Europeans in his country reduced this by 90%: a hard blow indeed. But though numerically and economically straitened, the Church of Alexandria has still kept the freedom and privileges enjoyed by other religions and confessions in Egypt.

The need for missionary endeavour on the African continent represents an opening that, on the one hand, makes up the numerical losses, but, on the other, requires funds and missionaries this Church, in its present situation, is unable to supply. In this respect, it has received outside aid on a generous scale, especially from the Greek Church. It should be noted that the Greeks, having had nothing to do with colonialism, are well received in Africa. This help has led to a growing number of new missionary centres, and a parallel increase in the number of converts and indigenous priests, a vital new element for the Church of Alexandria, which now embraces Greek and Arab Orthodox, the old inhabitants of the continent and new emigrants.

The Patriarchate of Antioch

The jurisdiction of this Patriarchate in the Near East extends to Syria, with six dioceses, Libya, also with six, Mesopotamia and the Arab Chersonese, with one, and Turkey, with three, all *sede vacante*. The hostile attitude of the latter has led to the dispersal of the faithful from their respective regions and the removal of the Patriarchal See from Antioh to Damascus. The upheavals the region has suffered—the Arab-Israeli wars and the civil war in Lebanon—have caused serious hardships for the Patriarchate. The *ethno-philetic* criteria (the imposition of national-racial standards on the make-up of the Church) prevailing in the latter part of the nineteenth century in the life of the Church of Antioch, produced an internal crisis and led to its relative enfeeblement. The Russian Orthodox Church sought to take advantage of this situation, and in order to consolidate its influence, instituted a Patriarchal *apocrissary* in Damascus.

Together with the other eastern Patriarchates, that of Antioch witnesses to the values of Orthodoxy in Muslim lands. Besides its strictly pastoral works, with 410 parishes and 300 parish priests, it has important educational and charitable responsibilities, with several impressive institutions in being to serve these ends. The Church takes care of half the subsistence of its officials, from the offerings of the faithful and the revenues from its properties, which are held under the statutes of the *vacuf*.

The Patriarchate of Jerusalem

This is a special case: the Patriarchate is completely contained in the monastic community which forms the *Ieron Koinòn* (Holy community) *of the Most Holy Sepulchre*. Its jurisdiction extends to Palestine-Israel, Jordan and the Chersonese of Sinai.

The Patriarchate exists in an epicentre of disturbances, a crossroads of peoples and religions, an object of international diplomatic moves. This is why it has played its part in major historical events and why the trials of the past and the present remain stamped on its life. With a community of faithful of Greek and Arab provenance and very limited financial means, the Patriarchate of Jerusalem remains the custodian of the most precious relics of Christianity, of which the Holy Sepulchre is the most precious of all.

It meets its expenses from the offerings of the faithful and from revenues from its property—what is left of it after the loss of its possessions in Russia, Rumania and Turkey, and the lien held on the rest as a result of the Arab-Israeli war. It still has to maintain its monks and clergy, preserve sacred monuments of enormous value, and support about fifty primary and secondary schools, with 150 teachers and 2500 pupils, either Greek or Arabic-speaking, which cost some $45,000 per annum. But it is the sanctuaries of the Holy Land that are still the pride and treasure of the Patriarchate of Jerusalem, to be guarded like the apple of its eye.

Note. All these ancient Patriarchates, now more or less needy, can count on the moral and material help of Greece by virtue of their common bonds of historical and spiritual parentage. Amongst the forms of aid they receive are, principally: exemption from public taxes and from the compulsory expropriation of property they hold in Greece; grants for the conservation of their historical monuments, works of art, libraries, etc; help in their educational work, in the form of bursaries, etc; payment to the bishops and priests of the dioceses of the Ecumenical Patriarchate in Greece (Crete and the Dodecanese: thirteen dioceses and 1,000 parish priests); and special support for Mount Athos. All this given in a spirit of fraternal solidarity.

The new Balkan Patriarchates

The existence of the Patriarchates of Serbia, Rumania and Bulgaria—leaving aside what happens in the Soviet Union—demonstrates how the Orthodox Church survives in Communist countries and how it co-exists with regimes opposed to religion on principle. One must admit that this is achieved by compromise: the political regimes have in fact had to make concessions in order to avoid the fatal error of conflicting with the religious consciousness of the people, for whom religion is an integral part of national institutions. The Yugoslav regime made a maladroit attempt to use the Church for political ends by setting up, and with no canonical sanction, the so-called 'Macedonian Church' in 1967. This was done as a part solution of the whole 'Macedonian question.' The separation of this 'Church' from the Patriarchate of Serbia was officially condemned by this Patriarchate itself and by the whole of the Orthodox Church.

It must be said, however, that the policies of these states toward the Church is not simply one of tolerance: they give it legal status, support, facilities, in some cases virtually privileges. Even under Communist regimes, the Patriarchates, dioceses and parishes can keep goods and properties, have the right to levy taxes and contributions, to accept donations, bequests and hereditary legacies, to have institutes, meeting-places, workshops for sacred articles with the necessary sales outlets, printing works and bookshops for religious books. The Church administers its revenues at its own discretion, under its own control and on its own responsibility, for ecclesiastical purposes (administration, seminaries, maintenance of clergy and religious, and other works). Above all this, of course, there is still the sovereignty of the State.[2]

The Church of Cyprus

The Apostolic Church of Cyprus is today, as it has done for centuries, experiencing the great struggle of its people for their freedom and self-determination. This struggle has been the dominant influence in the formation of its feelings and thought; it has given it leaders, such as the late Archbishop Makarios III. The rôle of mentor the Church plays in the island is proof of its vitality in both the spiritual and the economic spheres—both fruit of its efficient organization and administration and its consciousness of its own mission.

The Turkish invasion of Cyprus in 1974 led to the occupation and devastation of 42% of the land. Out of a population of 650,000 (of which only 1.8% were Greek Orthodox), more than 200,000 fled. The ravages spread from people to holy places, statues and other works of Christian art. The Church still remains bravely with the people, who are carrying on their hard struggle to survive and rebuild; at the same time it maintains close ties with the political powers to their common advantage.[3]

The Church of Greece [4]

Even though the constitution of the country guarantees the religious freedom of all 'recognized' faiths (Art. 13), the Greek Orthodox Church is still the official religion of the State; this is due to the fact that the overwhelming majority of the people (97%) profess the Orthodox faith, and because historically Orthodoxy has been synonymous with Greek national life, to the extent that the terms 'Greek' and 'Orthodox' are interchangeable in the minds of the people. The history of the Turkish domination and the Greek uprising of 1821 provide ample justification for this.

The Greek State recognizes the Church's right to self-government while at the same time looking for ways of collaborating with it in matters of common interest. This collaboration is also expressed through the recognition by the State of the Holy Synod's right to express its viewpoint officially on any ecclesiastical law to be voted in the Parliament. Equally, the State recognizes that the Church of Greece as a whole, and each diocese and parish, has a juridical existence in public law, affecting its juridical relationships, and exempts its properties from public taxes. Parish priests and deacons are paid by the State, which also contributes the major part of the bishops' expenses.[5] Furthermore, the State has taken on all seminary costs (at present there are some 2,000 seminarists), and the salaries of teachers of religion in public secondary schools (also about 2,000). It also promotes the teaching of theology by financing two theological faculties, at the Universities of Athens and Salonika. The State contributions to the Church also enable it to spend large sums on archaeological restoration and conservation of sacred monuments and works of art, in which Greece is extremely rich, and it also makes exceptional payments for works on churches and monasteries.

All these state favours to the Church are seen as compensation for the nine-tenths of its former lands, which the State has taken over at various times, and for the revenues it receives from and by means of the Church.[6] Not only this, but the State recognizes its obligation to help the Church in the enormous amount of social work it carries on throughout the country, through more than 600 foundations, and in its work of moral formation through its spiritual apostolate to the people.

The Church of Albania

The present situation in Albania strikes a discordant note in comparison with the condition of the Churches in the other Balkan States, even more so than that struck by the behaviour of Turkey toward the Ecumenical Patriarchate. The Orthodox Church in that country, which at the beginning of the last war had a membership of more than 250,000, of Greek origin, today lives under a regime of persecution. Officially, nothing is allowed to be known about its fate.

The intervention of the State in the internal life of the Church has produced an irregular situation; the canonical archbishop has been exiled and a new one set up anti-canonically in his place. This situation is not recognized by the Ecumenical Patriarchate, which had granted the Albanian Church its autonomy ('autocephalous' status) in 1937.

COMMENT AND PROSPECTS

Following this rapid survey of the present situation of the Orthodox Churches in the Near East, one needs to ask what their prospects are for the future in the light of a present so full of problems.

1. The Patriarchate of Constantinople is going through the most critical phase in its long history. The intolerant policies of Turkey hold it in a vice-like grip. This critical situation coincides with the forced migration of the Greek-Orthodox population from Turkey and the eventual dispersal of the hierarchy from Constantinople. Let us not be any too

optimistic about its succession. But what will actually happen? Will Turkey actually take this last, fatal step? If it does, which God forbid, humanity will for the third time bewail the fall (*alosis!*) of Constantinople. Will the civilized world allow such a thing to happen? Everyone must share the responsibility for this sad story. Meanwhile, the spiritual prestige of the Ecumenical Patriarchate—despite its material enfeeblement—remains unaltered, and it still holds the first place among the Orthodox Churches.

2. As for the Patriarchate of Alexandria, the missionary endeavour to the black continent shows it the way to the future. Natives of Africa are taking the place of the tiny Greek population. New times, new men. Institutions with a solid spiritual basis can survive historical changes.

3. The Patriarchate of Antioch is today torn between the old Graeco-Syrian tradition and the influence the Russian Church is trying to exert on it. Yet, in the midst of the trials it is undergoing as a result of the wars, it has to choose its way forward. Will it make the right choice? Whether it will remain true to its traditions or finally submit to pressure from the North remains to be seen.

4. The Patriarchate of Jerusalem finds its life and glory in its charge of faithful custodianship of the Holy Places; this great mission is tied to the fate of the Holy City, today contested between Israelis and Arabs.

5. At the present moment it would appear that the new Patriarchates of the Balkan countries have won the first round in the experiment of co-existence with communist regimes. They seem to be flourishing in the Communist 'paradise.' But they will have to do everything in their power to maintain, or even better, their position.

6. The Church of Cyprus has gone through the crisis of the splitting of its hierarchy, through political motives, at the time of the Turkish invasion. Now it needs to bring the two sides back together. It has the strength to do so, but needs the support of all men of good will.

7. The Church of Greece is faced with a number of problems, of which two stand out. First, it has to win back its popular following lost during the period of the dictatorship (1967–74) through the rash collaboration of many of its leaders. Second, it must prepare for eventual separation from the State, an event which Parliament has recently been debating. This is necessary because the *sensus ecclesiae,* in both clergy and people,[7] requires a 'new look,' with an efficient administration, reorganized economic means, a reassessment of all its strengths and true, coherent policies.

8. As for the Church of Albania, we can only wait and see, hoping for some opening of the Albanian State to the world, which will allow a little light and air to penetrate to this suffering Church.

CONCLUSION

The Orthodox Church, as a living, healthy organisn, has always had the capacity to adapt and orientate itself to the signs of the times. It has lived, and still lives, without changing its character or abandoning its course, continuing to give its witness with outstanding success. How is this achieved? Through its enormous spiritual strength, which makes even its limited means bear fruit. With the apostle, it can say of itself: 'It is when I am weak that I am strong' (2 Cor. 12: 10). This is the key to understanding its perennial vitality.

Translated by Paul Burns

Notes

1. Cf. *Annals of the Greek Parliament,* Session LVIII, 18 Jan. 1977 (Athens, 1977), pp. 2436–47, which reports the whole discussion on the fate of the Greek Orthodox in Turkey. The figures given there speak for themselves: in 1917 the Greek Orthodox population of the country was five million; today, despite international guarantees, between two and three in every thousand are left! This astonishing decline is hardly accidental.

2. Cf. Arts. 189 and 190 of the *Statute on the Organization and Functioning of the Orthodox Church of Rumania* (1948), and Art. 209 of the *Constitutional Charter of the Church of Bulgaria* (1950). These show that the Patriarchate of Rumania had 8,828 parishes, 9,821 priests and over 2,000 monks and nuns in 74 monasteries and convents; the Patriarchate of Bulgaria had 3,200 churches and 500 chapels, 2,000 parish priests, 400 monks and nuns in 123 monasteries and convents.

3. The State, in compensation for goods taken from the Church, has taken on a large percentage of the salaries of the parish priests of the island, except those in city parishes, whom the Church itself pays. Cf. inter alia, Art. 110, para. 1, of the *Constitution of the Republic of Cyprus* (1960), which grants the Church of Cyprus: 'the exclusive right to order and administer its internal affairs and its goods, according to the sacred canons and its Constitutional Charter.'

4. The term 'Church of Greece,' by reason of its use (however inexact) in legislative, administrative and literary language, has become a technical term, referring to a specific juridical entity comprising the sum of those ecclesiastical dioceses in Greek territory which come, according to the Patriarchal and Synodal *Tomos* of 29 June 1850, and the Patriarchal and Synodal *Acts* of July 1866, May 1882 and 4 Sep. 1928, under the jurisdiction of the Orthodox Holy Synod resident in Athens. This excludes Crete, the Dodecanese and Mount Athos, which are dependent on the Patriarchate of Constantinople. This division of ecclesiastical administration in Greece does not seem to create any problems.

5. The 1977 budget provides $37,200,000 for the stipends of priests (8,200 for 8,300 parishes in the whole of Greece) and deacons (240 ordained out of 935 planned), and $1,200,000 for the maintenance of bishops.

6. The State takes 35% of the gross income of parishes, besides considerable sums from certain acts performed by the Church, such as marriage.

7. It should be borne in mind that the *people* play an active rôle in the life of the Orthodox Church. They participate in Diocesan as well as Parish councils, and in some Churches (Alexandria, Serbia, Romania, Bulgaria, Cyprus) also in the election of the hierarchy.

Bibliography

1. *Year Book of the Church of Greece for the Year 1977* (in Greek). Contains information on all the Orthodox Churches.

2. "Apostolos Barnabas," in *Rev. of the Church of Cyprus* 34 (1973), p. 304.

3. Barnabas Tzortzakos, Metropolitan of Kitros, *The Basic Administrative Institutions of the Orthodox Patriarchates* (Athens, 1972, in Greek).

4. Idem., *The Basic Administrative Institutions of the Autocephalous Church of Cyprus* (1974) (though a new Constitution is being prepared); Tzortzakos also examines the administrative institutions of the churches in Antioch (1973), Albania (1975), and Greece (1977).

5. *Constitution of Greece,* 9 June 1975, Arts. 3, 13, 18 and 105.

6. *Official Documents on the Administrative Status and Sanctuaries of the Church of Jerusalem* (Jerusalem, 1944, in Greek).

7. Konidaris Ger., *History of the Greek Church,* II (Athens, 1970, in Greek).

8. Law of 22 July 1968, n. 469. On the scale of remuneration of parish clergy of the Church of Greece (Gazette of the Govt. of the Kingdom of Greece, n. 162, 24 July 1968, fasc. A).

9. Law of 4 March 1975, n. 11. On taxes on property, etc. (Gazette of the Govt. of the Republic of Greece, n. 34, 5 Mar. 1975, fasc. A, art. 5).

10. Law of 4 March 1975, n. 12. On modifications and supplements to the system of payments (ibid., art. 24).

11. Maximos, Metropolitan of Sardi, *The Oecumenical Patriarchate in the Orthodox Church* (Thessalonica, 1976), pp. 300 ff.

12. Stavridis Bas, *Histoire du Patriarcat Oecumenique* (Istina, 1970), II, pp. 131–273.

Giuseppe Alberigo

A Constitution for the Restoration

BETWEEN 1971 and 1972 a fruitful discussion took place as to whether or not it would be opportune for the Catholic Church to give itself a fundamental law (cf., *Concilium*, 1971, No. 6). The debate began when a draft version of the Lex Ecclesiae Fundamentalis (LEF) was sent to all the Catholic bishops by the Pontifical Commission for the Revision of the Code of Canon Law. At this point two questions were put to the bishops: whether it was opportune for the Church to draw up a fundamental law as the theological and juridical basis of her various laws, and whether the draft version they had received could be considered adequate.

Thirteen hundred bishops (that is 40%) responded to the questionnaire; only 593—or 18%—accepted the principle, and only 61—that is 2%—accepted the draft version unconditionally.

Even the president of the Commission took tacit note of this catastrophic result and applied himself to an overall recasting of the text of the draft. The official report of the bishops' observations has never been published: all that is known of it is the summary report (*Communicationes* 1972, 122–160) which Mgr Onclin drew up without stating precisely the exact weight of the various opinions and with the transparent purpose of emphasizing the fact that the bishops' points of view conflicted with one another and were consequently mutually exclusive, thus leaving the Commission free to proceed in its own way. However, in June 1976 the drawing up of a new draft was completed, and this was sent, towards the end of 1977, to the cardinals who belonged to the Commission for the Revision of the Code of Canon Law, so as to enable them to give their opinion. The outcome of this consultation is not known.

Today it is possible to make a comparision between the version voted on by the bishops in 1971 and that of 1976. Materially the draft is a little shorter; many canons have been left as they were, but their position in the text has been changed. At the end of the present version four canons (83–86) have been added. These are concerned with the definitive norms on the nature of the LEF, its relationship to the canonical code and the procedure for its modification.

Here in this article we are concerned to see whether the new text, assuming an essentially juridical character, has really eliminated the theological elements, and also to assess the influence of the episcopal consultation which took place in 1971.

One preliminary observation: the legislative section of the LEF should be preceded by a theological-canonical introduction, one version of which was discussed during the seventh session (*Communicationes* 1974, 60–72). The text that has been made available to us bears no trace of it, and from the minutes of the other sessions there is nothing to suggest an adequate reason for its absence.

Canons 1–8 on the Church and the call to join it reveal that an effort was made to eliminate the 'theological' parts (canons 1, 1b; 1, 2; 1, 4) which refer specifically to the Church as the People of God. In this connection the perhaps more delicate question presents itself: is it realistic to persist in trying to separate ecclesiology from law about the Church? According to what criteria can one state that 'People of God' is a theological category, while 'Church,' on the other hand, is a juridical category? And is there not a danger that, involutarily perhaps, the distinction might become instead a distinction between pre-Vatican II ecclesiology and the ecclesiology of Vatican II? Were this the case, it would be difficult to believe that the demands of the bishops followed such a trend, rather than that—diametrically opposed to it—which, confirmed by John XXIII and Paul VI, envisages an adaptation of canon law to the ecclesiology taught by the council.

The unity of the Church is stated in such a way as to ensure that the Bishop of Rome and the Curia have control over all the other churches. The principle of subsidiarity, admitted verbally (*Communicationes* 1974, 62) has not been respected. The distinction between clergy and laity is restated with absolute disregard for the contemporary rediscovery of the significance and the traditional richness of the ministerial structure of the Church as a whole. As a result, for example in canons 60–70, which are concerned with the *munus sanctificandi,* there is no mention of the common priesthood of the faithful, and their share in the *munus sanctificandi* is reduced to *ministeria si quae receperint exercendo,* to participation in the liturgy, to prayer and to works of charity (canon 67, 4). Of their possible prophetic ministry, of the theologico-scientific magisterium, of counsel, and so on, that is to say of all the richly various manifestations of ministry, there is no mention at all, because they do not enter into the verticalist perspective adopted by the LEF.

A second novelty is contained in canon 2: this deals with the place reserved for 'ritual churches,' that is, to the various rites which exist, above all, in the East, whose constitution in ecclesiastical provinces and patriarchates is envisaged. This is the result of the contribution to the work of the Commission of experts in oriental canon law—but the significance of the contribution is diminished by the fact that the space accorded to regroupings of particular churches (bishops' conferences) in the Latin church, is reduced.

Canons 3–8 are devoted to a consideration of the relationship between the Church and mankind. This consideration is made in an individualistic key: account is taken of individuals, but not of their human groups or their religious communities. These canons too have been de-theologized, with the net result that membership of the Church no longer has anything to do with incorporation into Christ or a relationship with the Holy Spirit! In canon 6 baptism is said to incorporate one no longer into the *ecclesia Christi* but into the *ecclesia catholica.* In canon 7,1 the reference to the People of God has been retained, and it is stated that all baptized Christians belong to it, even those outside the Catholic Church, but—it is specified—*aliqua ratione.* It is impossible to see what significance this addition can have, unless it is a restrictive one—in contrast to the explicit teaching of Vatican II (*Lumen Gentium* 15; *Unitatis Redintegratio* 3). The basic idea of the LEF remains that of the Church as 'the perfect society'; thus the LEF as it has been formulated does not respond to the task of translating into juridical terms the theological teaching of Vatican II, since it removes the declarations of the council from their context and forces them into a different and in some ways incompatible framework.

Canons 9–28 are concerned with the rights and qualifications of the faithful. It is in this section that the 'juridical' orientation of the new version should have borne fruit, satisfying demands for a formulation of 'the rights of the Christian.' One would expect to find an explicit statement of two great principles. In the first place that of 'Christian freedom,' which even ecclesiastical laws are meant to serve. Such a principle, placed at the top of the list of the 'rights of the faithful,' would have, apart from enormous psychological advantages, the effect of providing a basis and a criterion for the drawing up of such a list, removing the impression of empiricism and of its being adapted to civil legislation. Enunciation of the principle of subsidiarity would have had analogous significance from the social point of view.

Canons 29–39, which treat of the pope and of the episcopal college, no longer isolate the pope from the episcopal college, thus accepting one of the criticisms made in 1971. This is an indubitable act of conformity with the ecclesiology of Vatican II, but it, is nevertheless unable to disguise other modifications in the opposite sense. Canon 29 on the divine institution of the hierarchy introduces, in para. 1, the theological qualification of Jesus as *ecclesiae caput invisibile,* thus resurrecting the language of a particular late medieval school of theology which was concerned to exalt the monarchy of the pope. Par. 3 of the same canon is based on the preceding 39,1 and 40, but omits to mention the 'succession' of the episcopal college to the apostolic college, and the fact that the episcopal college is 'representative of the whole Church.' It is significant that while para. 1 of canon 29 says that Jesus Christ *voluit apostolos, eisque praeposuit Petrus,* the two succeeding paragraphs reverse the relationship: first the pope is mentioned (par. 2), then the rest of the bishops (par. 3).

Once the priority of the personal power of the pope has been established, the LEF regulates the exercise of other powers as a consequence of it, restricting itself to a distinction between a *personal mode of exercise* and a *collegial mode of exercise* of the supreme power which resides in the pope. Within the terms set by the LEF there exists no *ius episcoparum* for the government of the universal Church, which should be respected by the pope, but only a *ius episcoparum uti singuli* for the government of individual churches, and it is this that the supreme authority of the pope must respect and protect (cf. canon 29, par. 2). That is to say that the responsibility proper to the episcopal college has no corresponding *ius.* Following Vatican II, the 1971 version (canons 49 par. 1, 46 pars. 1 and 2) made the provision that, both in ecumenical council and in its dispersed state, the episcopal college should be able to exercise its authority in the Church, *even* without active participation on the part of the pope, however much the latter may confirm or freely accept such acts. This eventuality (typically juridical) is no longer provided for in the new text (even though there is no evidence that the commission ever discussed the proposition— *Communicationes* 1976, 103–104). Canon 35 par. 2, on the other hand, provides that there can be no collegial action of the dispersed episcopate unless at the formal initiative of the pope (according to *Communicationes* 1977, this paragraph had been rejected by the drafting committee). Among the reasons put forward for eliminating 'acceptance' of this possibility, the following risk was cited: that a thousand or so bishops could, for example, pronounce themselves in favour of a revision of the law of celibacy, and that at this point there would be nothing left for the pope to do but to excommunicate these bishops.

The orientation of this section of the LEF seems to be extremely clear: the practical liquidation of episcopal collegiality, understood as the possibility of any kind of initiative on the part of the bishops as a body, with respect to which the necessary complement of papal intervention would come after the event and not before. The body of bishops is invested with no right to take the initiative: everything proceeds from Rome in the form and in the manner determined unilaterally by Rome.

There follow three short sections devoted to the patriarchs (canons 40–42), to the bishops (canons 43–45) and to priests and deacons (canons 46–49). The first is new, as has been said, but it contains nothing new with respect to the weakened image used by uniate ecclesiology, so that the net effect of these canons is that they fit the venerable institution of the patriarchate into the pyramidal conception of the Church put forward in the LEF. The refusal to accept the idea of a patriarchate of the West presided over by the Bishop of Rome is significant (*Communicationes* 1977, 94 and 299–301).

As for the section *De Episcopis,* it should be noted that canon 43 par. 2 repeats par. 2 of canon 47 in the 1971 version, but with an addition relating to the cessation of communion between the pope and a bishop which would mean for the bishop (automatic?) forfeiture of his office. In the following section, a reference has been added to the duty of regular priests responsible for the cure of souls to depend on their local ordinaries.

In canon 51 par. 2 the perspective in which the Church figures as a prophetic presence at the heart of society is abandoned, the only concern being for its stabilizing function. In fact, among the conditions which enable the Church to *exsistere* as a recognized bond among the various communities and nations, the previous version included recognition on the part of the latter of the inalienable rights of man. This condition has disappeared, on the pretext that Christian values have exercised an influence of their own even where these conditions do not exist (*Communicationes* 1977, 100). The explanation is obviously not adequate, because the point at issue is not the witness of Christian values as such, but the recognition of the Church as *Persona*.

Canons 55–88 establish norms for ecclesial functions. The most crucial point is dealt with in par. 2 of canon 55, where, alongside the affirmation that the *tria muners* have a single end, it is argued that their unifying element is the *munus regendi!*—and the function of government becomes in effect the key element in the guidance offered by the

Church. In this deterioration is expressed all the unbroken logic of the LEF—consonant with the principle of its inspiration, as expressed in canon 1. This reduction of any kind of individuality of *potestas* in the Church to a pure logic of power is expressed in *Communicationes* 1973, 209 in an exemplary and lapidary way. With the suggestion of the rapporteur that at some point when the appropriate moment came, it should be stated that all power in the Church is service, 'all agreed, because service is, in effect, nothing more than the right to exercise power'(!)

A genuine novelty was constituted by the final norms (canons 83–86), in which some of the basic questions related to the LEF, which were never submitted to the episcopate for consideration, are decided. In fact, these four canons stipulate that the LEF applies throughout the Catholic Church (83); that the LEF prevails over every other ecclesiastical law or contrary custom and that all recognized laws and customs must be interpreted and applied according to the LEF (84); that the pope alone, in the actual event through the mediation of the appropriate court, will ascertain whether laws and customs conform to the LEF (85); that the supreme ecclesial authority can abrogate or suspend the norms of the LEF only by means of appropriate legislative acts (86).

In this way the supreme value of the LEF is stated unequivocally. It is expressly recognized as a *norma normans* against which every decision, even of early ecumenical councils, and every custom, however venerable, must be weighed. That would be enough to demonstrate the potentially disruptive effect of an LEF with respect to the *status ecclesiae,* which would emerge shaken and unrecognizable.

Never has such an assumption accompanied the adopting of any position whatsoever in the Church, even doctrinal. Even doctrinal positions claim not to innovate but to fit into the earlier tradition of the Church, within which they want to be interpreted. The LEF, on the other hand, is henceforth to constitute the supreme criterion for interpreting everything that has been established in the Church, both before it and after it.

Without repeating here the very copious observations which were formulated between 1970 and 1972 and which still retain all their value, it seems right to conclude this analysis by posing a number of questions:

(1) Can the modifications which characterize the new version be said to result from the wishes of the majority of the bishops, given that they appear to be dictated, without exception, by centralizing and authoritarian preoccupations?

(2) How can those things which have not been changed with respect

to the 1971 version be said to suit the bishops, considering only 61 gave their *placet?*

(3) Does not the very unsatisfactory result of six different versions drawn up over a period of ten years suggest that the idea of giving a fundamental law to the Church after 2000 years is immature, to say the least?

Translated by Sarah Fawcett

Statement about Puebla

THE celebration of the Episcopal Conference in Puebla urgently draws us closer to the life and reflection of that part of the Universal Church which is present in Latin America. We are fully aware that, above all, the Conference is the task of our Latin American brothers and sisters, but we also consider it a Church event which concerns us all. Indeed, Vatican Council II reminded us of the interdependence among local churches as an expression of the profound communion in the same faith and hope. Furthermore, this interdependence has been a rich ecclesiastical experience lived in different events during these last years. It is an experience which has shown us that communion does not mean the absence of challenges and questionings, nor does it exclude historical or present reproaches. On the contrary, it has made us better understand how a people, which are pilgrims in history, all along their path must continually convert themselves to the poor if they want to be faithful to their Lord. It is in this sense that Puebla concerns and questions us. In fraternally presenting our expectations we declare ourselves affected by this event. We do this because of what the Latin American Church means for us, and in this way we recognize its significance beyond continental limits.

Ten years ago, the Medellin Conference, in unforgettable terms and with prophetic spirit, shook the whole Church and raised hopes which are still burning. At that moment of the post-conciliar stage, when so many roads were open to the presence of the Church in the world, the voice of Medellin reminded us of the existence of those poor of the world, so often marginated and despoiled by the same modern world to

141

which the Church community optimistically was seeking to open itself. It was a call to see things from a point of view different from that which we are accustomed to, a radical call to go beyond every institutional adaptation and to confront ourselves with that which must be taken into account if we want to build a Church of the poor, a Church faithful to the liberating God, in solidarity with those whom he loved preferentially, the poor and oppressed. The post-conciliar period in Latin America traveled along roads which perhaps were not foreseen, but which are profoundly in accordance with the original intuitions of the thrust of the Council. Furthermore, if interdependence does not mean unilateral dependence, and if collegiality is not submission and mechanical repetition, then Medellin was a vigorous and challenging testimony of communion for the whole Church.

In these years, the life of the Latin American Christian community has made the new accents which the Word of God acquires vibrate when it is read out from the poor people, exploited and at the same time believing; a Word read out from the life and struggles of the poor who are freeing themselves from a social system which has oppressed them and impedes them from living as human persons. Medellin took up and gave new vigour to the experiences and voice of committed Christians in the process of liberation. The efforts to forge Christian communities rooted in the world of oppression and hope have deeply questioned us. The theology which comes from a faith and an experience of God which are lived in solidarity with the poor and in the liberating praxis, has enriched the Church's reflection.

The bishops who met in Medellin knew how to listen to the cry of the poor, and that is the source of Medellin's profound evangelical meaning, its options and its prophetic inspirations which have gone beyond Church boundaries and have marked the history of the Latin American people. For all of this, it is with indignation and rejection that we observed how those who, within and outside of Latin America benefit from the denounced social order, reacted by cruelly repressing every effort to build a more just society. The response to the desire to live with dignity was prison, torture and death. Among those who suffered this fate were many Christians—peasants, bishops, workers, students, priests—who are searching to announce the Gospel from the poor. This is the price of every prophetic attitude. The blood of those contemporary martyrs fecundates the Latin American land and gives testimony to the seriousness of the oppression which is lived there and which challenges every human person. Perhaps what is most scandalous in these facts is that this repressive violence is exercised by governments which claim to be Christian in order to defend what they consider to be occidental and Christian values. Faced with this situation there is no neutrality possible. It is a reality which affects and questions everyone. And it calls us not only to solidarity with what is happening in Latin America, but above all, to an urgent task within our own societies and to a demanding responsibility within our very own Churches.

The years following Medellin which are rich in experiences, creativity and testimony of the Latin American Church, and which now place us before the threshold of Puebla have also been years full of sufferings and searchings. The pressures of the powerful brought upon certain ecclesiastical groups, the fears of the unknown in these new experiences, the hostility against new theological currents, the diffidence and backward steps along the road which was begun have not been absent. Part of this has been expressed in some of the preparatory stages for the Puebla Conference. This has brought on frustration and uneasiness, and makes one think that instead of going on with evangelical audacity in the option which Medellin began to take up, the Latin American Church will take a step back.

We are convinced that such a regression would affect the whole Church and would damage the credibility which is necessary in order to announce truly and effaciously the Gospel in today's world. This would deny Christ's face in the poor who interpret our faith. 'Where unjust social, political, economic and cultural inequalities are found, there is a rejection of the Lord himself,' Medellin told us. Those inequalities are even greater today and the attempts to create a just society are ferociously repressed. The rejection of the Lord is indeed greater in our days. Medellin was able to speak with courage, but also with profound hope in the future, about the part of the responsibility which the Church itself has in the history of oppression and in the situation of misery and despoilment which is lived in Latin America. The whole Church shares this responsibility. Recently, for example, we have been the painful witnesses of the support from ecclesiastical circles in rich countries to the efforts to silence the voices which spring from a life and reflection shared with the poor of Latin America.

Not only do we hope that Puebla will confirm the lines of Medellin, which is what our faith makes us long for, but rather we hope Puebla will go further and mark a new stage in the option taken up. Ten years ago, the Latin American Church began to point out that the direction to take in order to build a Church of the poor was the direction of solidarity with the poor in their struggle for liberation. Our hope is that the Spirit which moves with that struggle will continue to be a guide 'towards the complete truth.'

The road is difficult; many are those who have died for announcing the good news to Latin America's poor and oppressed. We know that in this road, if we love our brothers and sisters and if we are in solidar-

144 STATEMENT ABOUT PUEBLA

ity with their thirst for justice, we are passing from the systematic violations of the poor peoples' rights, from death, on to the assertion of life and resurrection. What the poor people of Latin America are living today in the Christian communities committed to the poor is a challenge to the conscience of every Christian who runs the risk of accommodating him or herself too easily to an opulent society. But above all, it is a reason for a joy which is asserted in the midst of suffering, and for a renewed faith in the life of the resurrected which definitely conquers all death. With that Paschal joy and faith in Life we express our hope in the action of the Spirit in the Puebla Conference.

Members of the CONCILIUM Foundation:

> Antoine van den Boogaard
> Paul Brand
> Claude Geffré
> Hans Küng
> Johann-Baptist Metz
> Edward Schillebeeckx

Contributors

WILLIAM BASSETT is currently professor of law at the University of San Francisco. He was six years on the faculty of the School of Canon Law at the Catholic University, Washington, D.C. He has published many studies in canon law, civil law and legal history.

WALTER BAYERLEIN is a judge in Munich, Germany. He is a member of the common synod of the dioceses of the Federal Republic. Since 1976 he has been one of the four vice-presidents of the Central Committee of German Catholics. He has published on canon law, ethics and the synod.

MICHEL BRION is a member of the working group on the support of the clergy and the Church of the French episcopate. He has published books and articles on pastoral strategy and finance, on French religious life, on clerical salaries and the resources of the Church.

PAUL MICHAEL BOYLE is superior general of the Passionist congregation. He has served as president of the Conference of Major Superiors of Men in the United States. He is founder and chairman of the Board of Trustees of Stewardship Services, Inc., and Religious Communities Trust.

VINCENT COSMAO, O.P., was Dominican superior in Dakar in 1959–65 and founded the Lebret Centre for Faith and Development in Paris in 1972. He has published an introduction to *Populorum Progressio* and an important work on development and faith. He contributes to *La Croix*.

EDWARD J. KILMARTIN, S.J., is professor of liturgical theology at the University of Notre Dame. He is the author of numerous studies on the history and theology of the sacraments, especially the eucharist.

FREDERICK R. MC MANUS is editor of *The Jurist*, associate editor of *Worship*, and since 1958 has been professor of canon law at the Catholic University of America. His published works include studies of Holy Week rites, the revival of the liturgy and the rite of penance.

PHOTIOS NIKITOPOULOS is a Greek Orthodox layman. He has studied at the Lateran and at Louvain. He worked for the Greek Ministry of Education and Cults and teaches at the major seminary in Athens. He has published on official theological dialogue between the Catholic and Orthodox Churches.

WIM ROOD is a member of the congregation of the Sacred Heart. His post-doctoral thesis was on Comenius and the Low Countries. He studied Czech and Russian and since 1970 has been co-secretary of the Netherlands bishops conference.

JACQUES SCHMITZ is an atheist. He is a journalist on the *Volkskrant*, a progressive, social democratic daily. He also works for a journal specializing in Eastern European affairs.

LOUIS M. TROUILLER is a Dominican. He has been in charge of the finances of his province since 1972. He has published on the integration of the clergy into French social security provisions and on ethics.

KNUT WALF is a German priest and professor in canon law at the University of Nijmegen in the Netherlands. He has published on papal diplomacy and canon law.